Having Meaningful

(SOMETIMES DIFFICULT)

Conversations

WITH YOUR ADULT SONS & DAUGHTERS

Greg and Lisa Popcak

Published by The Word Among Us Press
7115 Guilford Drive, Suite 100
Frederick, Maryland 21704
wau.org

25 24 23 22 21   1 2 3 4 5

ISBN: 978-1-59325-555-8
eISBN: 978-1-59325-558-9

Design by Suzanne Earl

Made and printed in the United States of America

Library of Congress Control Number:
2021919088

Contents

A Note to Readers

Every parent dreams of having not only wonderful relationships with their adult children but also meaningful conversations with them across the years. We feel confident in saying that God wants this for you too, because God designed parents to be mentors for their children and signs of God's love for them. It is our prayer that this little book will give you the means to make that dream a reality.

How will we approach this topic? We'll give plenty of examples of conversations between parents and adult children, but we decided to avoid discussing specific topics, such as religion, politics, and lifestyle, in favor of laying out basic principles. We hope that this approach will give you, the reader, the confidence and ability to have meaningful conversations on a variety of topics while making your parent-child relationship stronger and deeper.

We've divided the book into three parts:

Part One, Preparing the Soil. Before you can plant the seeds for fruitful conversations with your adult children, you need to make sure the soil is ready. We'll consider how to heal any scorched earth in the relationship—damage that's come about through previous interactions between you and your adult children. Even if you're relatively confident that the relationship is solid and that the soil is ready, what practices will ensure that your meaningful conversations will fall on fertile ground?

Part Two, Planting the Seeds. In this section, we'll explore good communication and caretaking-in-conflict skills that effective parents use. These skills enable parents to successfully start meaningful conversations with their adult children and to keep those conversations going in a positive direction once they've started.

Part Three, Tending the Buds. We'll explore additional ways to keep conversations going and good relationships growing.

We've based the anecdotes we use on several sources: the calls we receive regularly on More2Life, our radio program that airs on the EWTN Global Catholic Radio Network and SiriusXM130; the conversations we have with our clients at CatholicCounselors.com, our Catholic telecounseling practice; the conversations we've had with parents who have successfully established relationships with their adult children; and research about what it takes to turn difficult conversations into productive ones.

Learning how to have meaningful and even difficult conversations with your adult children is a gift that keeps on giving. Whatever life throws at you and your adult child, you'll be ready for it if you know how to talk about it. You'll also know how to use it to make your relationship everything you want it to be and everything God has designed it to be.

PART ONE

Preparing the Soil

We'll explore the tools that will help Christian parents have meaningful conversations with their adult kids. Specifically, we'll discuss

- some common obstacles;
- praying for and with your adult kids;
- people, not projects: helpful attitudes for healthy conversations;
- the basis of influence: strengthening attachment with adult kids; and
- guilt vs. response-ability: how to get out of your own way.

CHAPTER ONE

Scorched Earth and Other Obstacles

Are you struggling to have respectful discussions with your adult children about difficult topics? If so, you're not the only one.

◆ ◈ ◆

My daughter and I have always been close, and we talk about most things, but recently she started dating a guy who is bad news. I don't want to hurt her feelings or create the impression that I don't trust her, but I think she's wearing rose-colored glasses. I don't know how to share my concerns without driving her away or making her double down on this relationship out of spite.

———— ◆ ◆ ◆ ————

My twenty-four-year-old son told me that if we won't let him stay in the same room with his girlfriend at our house, he won't visit us on holidays or vacations anymore. We've tried to talk to him about why this is so important to us, and he knows where we stand; but the conversations always break down, and we end up fighting. He says that he's an adult, he's "put up with our Catholic BS his whole life," and now it's our turn to respect what he wants.

I don't understand why this is so hard. We didn't raise him to be like this. He went to church with us his whole life. We sent him to Catholic school all the way up to college.

My husband and I are so hurt. How can he be so hostile? I don't know how to begin to have a productive conversation with him about any of this.

———— ◆ ◆ ◆ ————

My son and I always had a good relationship, but recently he won't talk about anything but politics. It always turns into an argument. The last time, he told me that he was tempted to never speak to me again for the way I voted in the last election. I just don't understand that. Why do these conversations have to be so painful?

———— ◆ ◆ ◆ ————

My thirty-two-year-old daughter cheated on her husband and told my wife and me that she wants to divorce him. They have two kids together! When we told her how disappointed we were in her and how irresponsible she was being, she hung up on us. Now she won't take our calls.

The other day, in reply to a voice mail I left, she messaged me to say that if we think so poorly of her, then we don't have to see her or the grandkids ever again. I can't believe she would be so cruel. How can we have any kind of conversation with her if she's going to be like this?

◆ ◆ ◆

When he was in college, my son, who is twenty-four, told me that he is gay. My husband and I love him very much, and we've tried to be there for him, even though he knows how upset we are. We encouraged him to be chaste—and we thought things were going OK until last week. That's when he surprised us by announcing on social media that he and his boyfriend (we didn't know there was a boyfriend) have been living together for almost a year and have set a date to get "married." We're just devastated—not to mention blindsided. He's been lying to us this whole time!

I don't know how to talk to him about this. I haven't said a thing. Our extended family—and even some of our other kids(!)—are falling all over themselves to congratulate him, but we feel sick inside. How can I help him see the long-term effects of his choices?

As parents, we'd like to think that our job is done when our kids leave the house. Having raised them, educated them, and given them a good start, we often assume that everything from that point forward should run on cruise control. And then reality hits.

Adult children don't always think the way we want them to think or live the way we want them to live. That shouldn't surprise us. Intellectually, we know it's possible, but it still feels like a punch in the gut when it happens.

How do we respectfully engage in conversations with adult children who don't think or believe as we do? How do we respond when our adult kids are passionate about ideas, or beliefs, or ways of living that are disagreeable, hostile, or downright antagonistic to our own? When our adult children start making choices that we believe—or know—are not in their best interest, how do we talk to them about it? How do we know when to speak and when to hold our peace?

Are there ways to have these conversations without having them blow up in our faces? And what if things have already exploded? Is there a way to repair the damage? More than that, is there a way to open our adult kids' hearts to the insights and wisdom we could offer—wisdom that might help them make better choices and save them from a world of pain?

These are the kinds of questions we'll address in this book. Although these situations are always delicate, often painful, and usually fraught, it is our privilege to accompany faithful parents like you as we navigate the land mines involved in dealing with adult children and the choices they make.

We hope that the stories we share and the recommendations we offer will prevent you and your children from taking a scorched-earth approach to difficult discussions. We'd like to help you instead have ongoing, fruitful conversations.

And the good news is that many faithful families do manage to have successful conversations about difficult issues. At their best, such conversations help parents and adult children draw closer to each other and give parents the ability to disciple their adult children on the path to more faithful, fulfilling lives.

The Seeds and the Soil

If you think of the conversations you'd like to have as seeds, then your relationship with your adult child is the soil. Is your relationship, generally speaking, fertile soil that allows your insights to sink in and take root in your adult child's life? Or is the relationship more like rocky soil or parched earth, in which the seeds die before they can germinate? When it comes to having meaningful or difficult conversations with your adult children, first you have to make sure your overall relationship is fertile soil. Then you can think about your message and the best way to put it across.

To this end, we will address three elements that will allow you to have meaningful and sometimes difficult conversations with your adult children: we'll help you cultivate the soil that is your relationships with your adult children, help you clarify what you want to say, and help you say it effectively. Addressing these elements will allow the best and most important parts of what you say to each other to sink in.

We begin by sharing some insights we've gained from working with parents who have been successful in having difficult conversations with their adult kids. Broadly speaking, there is one major pitfall they avoid and one major need they respect.

Major Pitfall: The Obedience Expectation

It can be hard sometimes to remember that, even though I'm still their dad, my kids don't have to do what I say. If I'm going to have any ability to be a positive influence in their lives, I can't insist that they listen to me. I can only invite them to listen—with my words and my witness.

—Jaime, father of three adult children

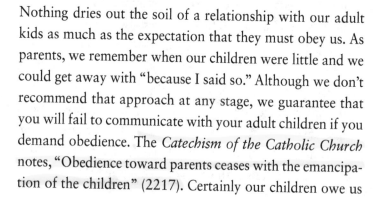

Nothing dries out the soil of a relationship with our adult kids as much as the expectation that they must obey us. As parents, we remember when our children were little and we could get away with "because I said so." Although we don't recommend that approach at any stage, we guarantee that you will fail to communicate with your adult children if you demand obedience. The *Catechism of the Catholic Church* notes, "Obedience toward parents ceases with the emancipation of the children" (2217). Certainly our children owe us their respect—just as any human being owes respect to others in a relationship. But our adult children are not obliged to do what we say.

Many callers to our radio program feel that the commandment to honor your father and mother (see Exodus 20:12) means that even adult children are obliged to defer to their parents' wishes, no matter what they are. But honoring your parents as an adult doesn't mean agreeing with everything they say or doing everything they want you to do. Primarily it means promising to provide for your parents in their old age and living in a manner that says, "That kid was raised right!" whether or not you actually were. Anything else is gravy.

Our kids don't owe us the sort of warm, close relationship we want with them. We have to be willing to build it. And when our children are not fulfilling their obligation to "honor" us in even a limited manner, commanding them to live up to their obligations doesn't do much good. The expectation of obedience is a poor substitute for an authentic relationship at any stage of parenting, and this is doubly true for the relationship we have with our adult kids.

As Christian parents, we have several privileges and responsibilities: We are responsible for attaching our children to us—helping them form a strong personal relationship with us. And we are responsible for evangelizing them—helping them form an intimate, personal relationship with Christ (see *Catechism*, 2223–2225 for more about this). These two privileged aspects of child-rearing go hand in hand. Parents are meant to reveal the loving face of God to their kids. By doing our best to help them feel attached to us, we allow them to experience—physically and emotionally—the love God has for them.

If we *effectively* attached our kids to us and evangelized our children to Christ as they were growing and if we continue to build our relationship with them and support their efforts to love and serve Christ as adults, we can reasonably expect that they will seek our input and advice and prayerfully consider what we have to say. But even in such a case, our adult children are not obliged to obey us.

At this point, many parents say, "But my adult child *isn't* connecting with me and [or] *isn't* listening to God!" If that's the case, then the problem isn't that they fail to listen to you. The problem is that something went awry somewhere along the way, perhaps in their childhood but perhaps simply in the choices they made as adults in spite of their upbringing.

Regardless, all the lectures in the world won't fix this. In fact, the more you lecture your adult children or demand that they listen to you—or for that matter, the more you avoid the subject altogether—the worse things will get.

Raising kids is tough, and trying to build a healthy relationship with adult kids can be tremendously difficult. Be that as it may, it doesn't do any good to beat yourself up or waste time wondering, "Where did we go wrong?" We'll discuss how to let go of misplaced guilt in chapter five. For now it's important to recognize two keys to an ongoing positive influence in your child's life: strengthening the attachment between you and your adult child and learning effective ways to evangelize your adult child. If you forget these essential elements and get caught up in arguing about

a specific choice, belief, value, or idea your child is espous-
ing, you will dig your own grave and leave your child with
nothing to do but count the minutes until it's time to buy
the headstone.

Successful parents of adult children know that any influence
they have is directly dependent on a strong connection between
parent and adult child and the depth of that child's relationship
to Christ. If the parent-child connection is breaking down, parents need to focus on shoring up these two elements—not on
developing better arguments and a harsher tone. The rest of
this book will show you how to shore up your ability to attach
and evangelize so that your child is more likely to hear you.

Major Need: The Longing for Parental Pride and Approval

*My parents and I have always had a difficult relationship. I
know they think of me as a major disapppointment. They're
superreligious, and I'm not. And yeah, I've struggled a lot, and
I've gone through some really bad times. I guess I understand
why they're frustrated with me.*

*But I'm a good person. I have a good job now. I'm respon-
sible. It's been hard, but I'm figuring it out, y'know? I just
wish—for once—my folks could say something good about
me or find something I've done that they could be proud of. I
can't talk to them because every time I do, I see they're always
going to be disappointed in me.*

—*Lane, thirty-eight years old*

◆ ◆ ◆

No matter how old our kids are, they'll always want our love. They'll always crave our approval, a word of encouragement, any sign that lets them know we think they're showing some strength, doing something right, or at least trying to pursue something worthwhile. No matter how damaged a relationship may be, every adult child wants to know that their parents are proud of them for *something*. We need to remember this.

Whether we're afraid to bring up a topic in the first place or we're trying to rebuild a relationship with a child who has turned their back on us, it's critical to find the good in what our adult child is trying to do—and to express our pride in the efforts they are making to pursue those good things. This is true even if we struggle with or disapprove of the way they are going about that pursuit.

◆ ◆ ◆

My daughter is pro-abortion. It kills me to see her advocating for abortion rights. We fight about it all the time. It used to get really ugly, to the point where we almost couldn't stand to be in a room with each other.

One thing that has helped in these conversations is that I took the time to understand her motivations. One day, almost in exasperation, I asked her to help me understand what she sees that's good about being "pro-choice" (as she refers to it). I wanted to try to understand what experiences she's had that made her feel so favorable toward the pro-abortion position.

To be honest, it was scary for me to do that. I was a little afraid of what she'd say. But I'm glad I took the risk.

She told me that she had a friend in college who was dating an abusive guy. Her friend got pregnant, and her friend's very religious parents tried to pressure her into marrying the guy. She finally got her parents off her back and was able to escape the abusive relationship by having an abortion. Nobody was happy with her decision, but it was the only way she could finally get support for leaving her terror of a boyfriend.

I was able to tell my daughter how much I sympathized with her friend's situation and how much I respected her belief that no woman should ever be put in that position. In fact, I agreed with her that the pressure her family put on her was unconscionable.

To my surprise, this conversation changed the way we talked about the issue. While I am able to see the positive intention behind her advocacy of abortion, I can respectfully challenge her on her limited imagination. Instead of her hearing me say that I think women like her friend should be forced into abusive situations, she hears me saying that they deserve better than abortion. Pushing women into killing their babies removes the pressure on society to support the abused in more constructive ways.

My daughter doesn't believe that such support is realistic. But now when we argue about this issue, she can at least respect the fact that we're on the same page in wanting abused women to have the tools and support they need to live better lives. Instead of just writing me off as a religious nut, she can see my heart. And I can see hers.

This mother went out of her way to understand what positive motivations drove her daughter to advance an objectionable position. Once she understood where her daughter was coming from, the mother was even able to validate and support her daughter's compassionate heart while they continued to discuss what true compassion looks like. She didn't let the issue destroy her ability to demonstrate her love for and approval of her daughter. She found something about her daughter's position that she could approve of and began to build from there.

For the daughter, experiencing the generosity of her mother's approval enabled her to stay in the conversation and not see her mother's disapproval of abortion as a personal judgment on her.

This approach works for almost any disagreement you could have with your adult child, from the kind of car they want to buy, to the career path they want to pursue, to the types of relationships they have, to the ideals they uphold, to the faith they choose to practice, and even to the unhealthy habits they take up. We'll give plenty of examples of this skill throughout the book. For now it's enough to know that, despite appearances to the contrary, your adult children are desperate for your love and approval.

Oddly, the more contrary they appear to be, the more this tends to be true. Being able to have effective conversations with our adult kids directly depends on our ability to identify and affirm the positive motivations behind their disagreeable choices, even while working with them to explore other more mutually agreeable options.

The fact is, however, that our attempts to have meaningful conversations with our adult children can leave us feeling more than a little burned-out. We hope this book helps you change that dynamic for the better in your relationships with your adult children.

FOR PRAYER

Lord, I give my relationships with my adult children to you. Show me how to strengthen each relationship and how to lead them to you—not so much with my words, but by my witness and my loving heart. Lead me and guide me. Amen.

Holy Family, pray for us.

FOR REFLECTION

1. What insights have you taken from this chapter?

2. How have you tried to engage your adult children in conversations in the past? Were those efforts successful?

3. How might your approach change, based on the ideas presented so far?

CHAPTER TWO

How to Pray for (and with) Your Adult Child

Our children do not belong to us. This is one of the most important points for Christian parents to remember, no matter the age or stage of their children. Our children are on loan to us from God. They come from God and are destined to return to God. Everything we do for them or say to them needs to respect the fact that our children are God's children first.

That's why prayer has to be the most important part of any meaningful or difficult conversation you want to have with your adult children. In this chapter, we'll look at several ways prayer can help you set the stage for fruitful discussions.

Praying for Your Kids

Sadly, my kids have fallen away from the Church. I wish I knew how to talk to them about the faith, but such conversation tends to make them defensive, so I just keep it to myself. Of course, I pray for my kids every day. I say a daily Rosary for their intentions, and I ask God to open their hearts to him. I can't make them be faithful, right? All I can do is hope and pray.

❖ ❖ ❖

Sure, we know that we need to pray for our adult kids, but how we pray can make a difference. We don't mean to suggest that there's a magic prayer formula, some incantation you can recite to make God open your kids up to your influence. All prayers are avenues of grace—between you and God, between your adult children and God, and between you and your adult children.

But prayer is a conversation, and as you know from your conversations with people throughout the day, some conversations are more fruitful than others. Generally speaking, conversations on any level—human or spiritual—are more effective when we work hard to listen to what the other person is saying instead of focusing on telling the other person what we want.

Too often our prayers for our adult children sound a lot like this: "Lord, please change my kid." That's a prayer, certainly. And God is happy to receive that prayer. He's happy that you would bring your concerns to him. The problem with that prayer, however, is that it leaves *you* out of the equation. It brings your adult child to God, but it doesn't prepare you to hear what God might want to say to you, either about your child or about how you could approach your adult child more effectively.

When parents call us to discuss the difficult topics they need to address with their kids, we always suggest they begin to pray along these lines:

> Lord, please help me know how to approach [name] about [X] in a way that will let them hear what I'm trying to say. Help me listen well, not just to what they're saying but to the intentions behind their words. Help me share your love with them in everything I say and do, and help me show them that even when we disagree, I'm on their side.
>
> Show me how to work with [name] so that we can find answers that will glorify you, work for the good of each of us, and help each of us become everything you created us to be.

This isn't an official prayer of the Church—and we encourage you to use your own words. But look at the difference between this approach to prayer and the example that opened this section. Both represent beautiful and sincere efforts to pray for an adult child, but in the first prayer, the parent is in a powerless position. All that parent could do was sit back, keep doing the same thing they always did, and hope God would bring about a different result.

In contrast, the prayer we suggest enables parents to humbly bring themselves to God, knowing that God wants to move in, through, and with them to effect graceful change. These parents admit they don't know what to do or say, and they ask God to guide them

If the parent in the first situation has a negative experience bringing up a topic with an adult child, they may feel stuck even as they continue to pray for their child to change. But if a parent in the second situation has a bad experience discussing a topic with their adult child, they can bring that experience back to God in prayer, asking him to show them how to identify the next step, and the next, and the next. Each time this parent prays, they assume God wants to work in them, with them, and through them to effect the change they seek in the relationship. They do not passively ask God to change things for them. They ask God to change *them*, so that they may be more effective instruments of his grace in their adult child's life.

We proposed this approach to Eric in counseling. Eric is sixty-three and the father of three kids. His oldest son, Kyle (thirty-four), had been having marital problems. Here's what he told us later:

I adopted this approach for conversations with my son, and I have to say, it was eye-opening. It killed me to see him suffering, and I wondered if I could help. The thing is, in the past we did a lot of things together, but we didn't have many heart-to-heart conversations. We just weren't used to talking on that level. So whenever I'd try to bring up something about his mar-

riage and how things were going, he'd just get quiet and say, "I don't really want to get into it, Dad." What could I do? I felt helpless. And to be honest, I don't do helpless very well.

When I started praying as you suggested, the idea sort of popped into my head that I should invite him to do even more things with me but not say much of anything. Looking back, I'm pretty sure it was the Holy Spirit showing me a way in. I'd ask Kyle for help with some project at the house. He was happy for the excuse to get out of his house.

A couple of times, I took him out for coffee or a drink. I wouldn't bring up anything, but eventually the conversation would come around to the kids and stuff. He sort of opened up naturally after a while and told me a little bit about what was going on between him and my daughter-in-law.

My wife had researched the better marriage counselors in the area. I didn't say anything at first, but when he finally started talking about what he was going through, I was able to listen and put him in touch with a counselor Marjorie had found.

Marjorie and I had been through counseling a couple of times ourselves, and it made a big difference for us. Kyle didn't know that. He was suprised when I told him about it. He and his wife have been going to counseling a couple of weeks now, and he says that he feels that it's making a difference.

I don't think I ever would have thought to take that approach. I normally would have backed off and hoped he'd sort things out on his own, once he had told me that he wanted me to stay out of it. I feel that praying in this way allowed God to show me how to diffuse the tension and make it safe to go a little deeper.

I'm grateful that God used me to get my son and daughter-in-law the help they needed, and I'm just as glad that it seems like we're getting a little closer through this whole experience.

Although Eric and Kyle didn't have the kind of relationship that involved deep personal discussions, God showed Eric how to use the relationship they did have in order to be a blessing to his son. He also showed Eric how to bring in the difficult times he and Marjorie had been through as a means of encouraging Kyle. Instead of simply asking God to fix things, Eric humbly asked God to show him how to be an instrument of grace in Kyle's life. God took the simple tools Eric and Kyle had at hand and showed them how to build an answer to the tough questions they were facing.

Praying in Conversation

A second way to incorporate prayer into your relationship with your adult kids is to invite God—in real time—into your interactions with them. Many callers on our radio program struggle with how they can encourage their kids to pray or how they can pray with them. One of the hurdles these parents face is the notion that prayer is a formal affair—a Hail Mary, for example—rather than something simple and spontaneous. On the other hand, some parents approach prayer as primarily spontaneous.

Regardless, many adult kids aren't open to their parents' way of praying, and so the parents feel powerless to pray with their children at all. Other parents feel they must get their adult child's express permission before praying with them.

We suggest breaking out of all these self-limiting assumptions. In the first place, there are many different ways to pray. It's fine to have certain prayers or devotions that speak to us, but we must be open to the specific prayer forms that each situation will allow.

Secondly, prayer is as essential as breathing for Christians. Just as God wants us to breathe, he wants us to pray so that he can be part of our conversations. However, we do need to be sensitive to our children and to the moment, in order to decide how we invite him in.

The best way we've found to do this is to start a kind of spiritual side conversation with God. For example, imagine that your adult child is complaining about work. Make sure to take a moment to truly empathize with their struggles. Don't try to give advice (yet). Don't critique what they've done so far. Don't pick the details apart. Just empathize.

"I'm so sorry you're going through this. I wish I knew what to do to make it all easier. I'm really proud of how hard you're working to figure out what to do."

Then take a moment to see how your comment landed. If your adult child seems to feel supported, you might say, tailoring your prayer to the child and situation, "It's really hard for me as your mom to see you going through this and feel like there's so little I can do. I want to take a minute to ask God to bless you. 'Lord, please bless Joe. Help him know how to respond to this in a way that will enable him to be the amazing person you created him to be. Let him know how proud I am of him and how much you love him. Amen.' So what's going on the rest of your week?"

Do you see how that worked? Don't ask permission. Don't invite comment. Empathize genuinely from your heart (this can't be just a technique), pray, and get out.

This works with difficult conversations too. Imagine that things are starting to escalate between you and your adult child. You're feeling hurt, picked on, and more than a little defensive. Before you say another word, say something like "This is really hard. I need to pause for a second. 'Lord, we both know what we want out of this situation. Help us work together to figure out what you want for us. And help us take good care of each other while we sort this out. Amen.' Alright, thanks for hanging in here with me. I guess what I'm hearing you say is . . . "

Again, the parent in this example doesn't make a big deal out of prayer. They just casually invite Jesus to be part of the interaction and then move on.

The advantage to this approach is that it shows humility: you aren't asking God to change your child; you're asking for help with a particular situation. Further, this approach helps you consecrate the situation to Christ in the moment, as opposed to toughing it out and then praying alone later.

Finally, assuming your prayer is received well and happens somewhat regularly, your son or daughter will start to experience prayer as a meaningful, tangible, connecting experience that you share together. It can form the basis for many deeper conversations, giving you even more ways in.

Some adult children who are hostile to God or to their parents' faith may find this objectionable, but adult kids often appreciate the extra prayer support, even if it doesn't mean exactly the same thing to them as it does to you. If your child asks you, "What was that about?" you can just say that you're learning to invite God into the little moments of your daily life so that you don't forget to pray about important things later. If your adult child voices more strenuous objections to this practice, you can back off and pray on your own. That said, we think you'll find it was worth the risk.

The takeaway from this chapter is this: don't be afraid to invite God into the exchanges you have with your kids. Do be sensitive. Make sure you empathize and provide genuine emotional support first. But given these conditions, don't feel that you must apologize or ask permission to pray for or with your child. Make it as casual, meaningful, and brief as you can, then move on. Let the Holy Spirit keep working behind the scenes in both of you.

FOR PRAYER

Lord, help me know how to make you part of every aspect of my relationship with my adult child. Show me how to bring your love, your grace, your wisdom, and most of all your heart to every interaction with my child. Make me a parent after your own heart, the parent my kids need me to be. Amen.

Holy Family, pray for us.

FOR REFLECTION

1. What ideas about praying for and with your adult kids stood out for you in this chapter?

2. How do the ideas in this chapter challenge or confirm your current approach to praying for and with your adult children?

3. What suggestions from this chapter would you most like to try with your adult child? Make a plan. When would you be most likely to have an opportunity to try to pray with your child? What will you do? What objections or comments might you expect? How would you deal with them gracefully?

CHAPTER THREE

People, Not Projects

In our counseling work, we often find that parents of young children view parenting not so much as a relationship they have with their children as a set of techniques they use on their children. Parents tend to assume that—barring a complete breakdown in family life—they automatically have good relationships with their children. It doesn't always occur to them—and even less to children—that the parent-child relationship is something that needs to be consciously developed, maintained, and deepened.

It's unwise for parents to presume a good relationship with their children at any stage. The relationship is only as good as the intimacy and openness it exhibits.

❖

Ellen called our radio program complaining about her twenty-seven-year-old son, Josiah. She was frustrated because he was no longer attending church. She thought he was also engaging in practices—especially in his dating relationships—that were contrary to the Catholic faith, in which she and her husband had raised him. Worse, she said that any time she tried to discuss these issues with him, he dismissed her, saying things like "That's really none of your business, Mom. I'm not going to discuss that with you."

We asked Ellen about her general relationship with Josiah, and she said she felt that, save for these issues, they had a good relationship. We asked her to describe what that looked like in practice. She mentioned that they usually talked once a week (she typically initiated these calls) and that they didn't argue unless she brought up these difficult topics. She also saw him about once every six weeks or so for family functions and at holidays. She mentioned that they didn't talk or text much in between, and that was because he was busy.

Ellen couldn't understand why Josiah was so closed to her when she tried to bring up his lifestyle.

◆ ◆ ◆

We were able to walk Ellen through a couple of formulas that helped her see what needed to change if she wanted to have meaningful conversations with her son. In essence, here's what we said.

When the depth of the questions we ask are *greater than* the depth of the relationship we have with our adult kids, we will encounter resistance. By contrast, when the depth of the questions we wish to discuss are *less than or equal to* the depth of the relationship we have with our adult kids, we will most likely find that they are willing to be open to us. For the mathematically inclined, here's what that looks like:

Depth of Questions > Depth of Relationship $\rightarrow$ Resistance.
BUT
Depth of Questions < OR = Depth of Relationship $\rightarrow$ Openness.

In short, the conversations we want to have with our adult kids need to fit into the relationship we have cultivated with them. Sometimes a relationship—though pleasant—can be too small to comfortably fit the big questions we want to discuss. It's like buying a couch that's twice as big as your living room. It's a great couch, but trying to make it fit is going to be awkward, at best.

This is why it's so important to work harder on your relationship with your adult kids than on the things you want to say to them. This can be difficult for parents to accept, not only because parents tend to assume that their relationships with their adult kids are better than they are but also because they assume that the work of raising them counts for more than it actually does. As with any relationship, our relationships with our adult kids require work.

No doubt this is frustrating for parents. Most parents of adult kids unintentionally behave like would-be gardeners who want to plant a tree. They go to the nursery, pick out a tree, and ask the gardener what they need to do to plant the tree. The gardener says, "Well, first you have to dig a really big hole."

The parents say, "Why are you talking about digging a hole when we want to grow fruit? We want the good stuff, but you're telling us we have to fuss about with the dirt."

The gardener says, "Well, . . . yes."

In our metaphor, the fruitful tree represents the conversation the parents want. The big hole is the relationship the parents need to "dig" to contain the conversation. Too often, when parents of adult kids call our radio program or come to us in counseling, they become frustrated when we tell them that they need to dig a big hole before they can plant their tree. They want us to show them how to prop the tree against their house and have it start producing fruit. That's not how trees work.

When the magnitude of the topics we wish to discuss with a child exceeds the depth of the relationship we have with them, we end up in a similar predicament. We can't plant the tree of fruitful conversation without digging the hole of a nurturing relationship. Without that hole, the person on the receiving end of our efforts can feel as though we're treating them as a project rather than seeing them as a person.

In his book *Love and Responsibility*, Karol Wojtyla (Pope St. John Paul II) argued that human beings have a God-given, built-in need to be loved as persons, to feel accepted. In daily life, we tend to be open with people when we feel they're more interested in being with us than in fixing us. When someone treats us in a less than personal way or uses us or tries to fix us, it triggers an emotional alarm within. This alarm (which

Wojtyla identified as a feeling of shame) drives us to put distance between us and that person.[1]

It can be frustrating to see our children making poor choices or their lives needing fixing. But the point isn't that we must stop giving our adult kids advice or offering help or that we must not ever say anything that could be construed as negative. The point instead is that we must be sure that any advice, help, and comments we offer don't come off like "You really are making a hash out of this part of your life. If you'd just get out of the way and let me handle it or if you'd just do what I say, everything would be fine."

The help we are trying to offer may be 100-percent correct. But our adult children will rightly experience this belittling approach as a violation of their God-given free will. And they will push against it.

Even God, our heavenly Father, respects the limits he established when he gave us the gift of free will. God wants to be involved in every decision we make, every thought we think, and everything we do. But he never intervenes unless we give him express permission to do so. He might find subtle ways to encourage us to seek help. If that fails, he might set up circumstances that make it difficult for us to avoid asking for help. But he never jumps in where he is unwelcome. God is always standing by our side, ready to offer grace, help, and counsel the second it looks as if we are willing to receive it. Until that moment, if we'd prefer to handle something on our own, he allows us to do that—even when it isn't in our best interest.

Meddling in someone else's life and choices or offering unsolicited opinions about their choices does not work for their good, no matter how well-intentioned the effort might be. When we speak to our adult children in a condescending manner, even without meaning to, we end up treating them like broken objects that need to be fixed, instead of like capable persons who need to be loved and understood.

Think about times when people you knew well overstepped their bounds and gave you unsolicited advice or questioned your judgment. Can you name even a single instance when you welcomed this? Probably not. There may be times when you realize you should have listened or even times you're glad you listened, but that's different from welcoming the input in the first place.

If you get a lot of pushback when you bring up a difficult topic with your adult child, that could be a sign that your relationship isn't as deep or healthy as you assume. Step back from the topic for a time, and work on strengthening the relationship. Then, as the relationship improves, you might raise the issue again.

In fact, this is exactly how God our Father approaches us, his adult children. We mess up all the time. Who among us wouldn't benefit from constant godly counsel? But the truth is, most of us wouldn't readily accept it. We want to do things our own way.

And what does our heavenly Father do? Does he swoop down, push us out of the way, and say, "You're doing that all wrong. Get out of the way"? Does he yell, "What do you think you're doing?" Or "You need to listen to me"?

No. Instead, he makes the tools of success (the Scriptures, the teachings of the Church) readily available, letting us know where to find the answers when we're ready. Then he relates to us in all the ways we allow him to relate to us and stands by, reminding us that he's there whenever we're ready to invite him into other parts of our lives. He wants to give us eternal life, but if the only time we ask for his help is when we've lost our keys, he'll happily start there.

The Shepherd's Heart

So where do we go from here? We're not God, but the good news is that we can follow his example.

◆ ◆ ◆

Mel was heartbroken when his forty-year-old son, Nick, left the Catholic faith and married Jenny, his second wife, without benefit of an annulment. His second marriage isn't valid in the eyes of the Church, and Nick and his wife now attend a local nondenominational Christian church.

When Mel tried to address these concerns directly, his son was patient but dismissive. Nick often said things like "Dad, I'm just not in the same place you are. I don't need all those rules to love Jesus."

Mel and his wife, Carol, came to counseling looking for ways to deal with their sense of guilt over their "failure" to raise Nick to be a faithful Catholic. They wanted to explore ways they could do more to address their concerns about both their son's spiritual life and his marriage outside the Church.

We asked Mel and Carol how often they discussed faith and religion or even prayed with Nick before he left the Church and married again. "Really, never" was their answer. They assumed that because they took Nick to church when he was a kid and sent him to religious education, he would naturally want to stay Catholic. They were shocked when it didn't work that way.

We suggested that, for now, the most important thing was to work on making the relationship deep enough to address the topics they wanted to discuss with Nick. We looked at ways that they might be able to more naturally start to engage in faith-sharing activities and religious discussions with him— not with an agenda, but to sincerely share this part of their life with Nick and Jenny.

Nick wasn't open to attending events at their parish, but he was fairly involved in the life of his new church. Worship at Nick's church was more charismatic and involved Scripture readings, preaching, praise, and contemporary Christian music. As far as Mel and Carol could tell, there wasn't anything anti-Catholic about Nick's church. Both Mel and Carol felt secure in their Catholic faith, and so we suggested that they tell Nick they wanted to learn more about his church.

Mel and Carol faithfully attended Mass, but they also made an effort to attend Nick's church a few times a month and go out to breakfast afterward. They also went to some social events at the church. They looked for opportunities to pray with Nick and Jenny, something they had never done before. It took some effort on Mel and Carol's part to become com-

fortable with spontaneous prayer, but doing so helped them deepen their spiritual connection with Nick and Jenny.

When Mel and Carol's parish offered a parish retreat, they invited Nick and Jenny, who surprised them by agreeing to attend.

Mel and Carol still have a long way to go to see the fulfillment of their dream of Nick and Jenny coming into the Church, but they felt more optimistic as they developed the spiritual side of their relationship. As they said, "We never had conversations like this before with our son, and we never prayed with him like this. What it took to open up to each other on this level was Nick's leaving the Church. We wish that hadn't happened, but we can say we feel closer to each other and God than we ever did before.

"Of course, we want Nick and Jenny to discover the beauty of the Catholic faith and have the marriage God wants for them, but we see God working in their lives. It's really nice to be able to share that and trust that God is calling us all to something deeper. I guess we just have to keep putting in the time, building the relationship, and trusting God to show us the way."

◆ ◆ ◆

Mel and Carol were smart to realize that lecturing or nagging Nick and Jenny about their faith life wouldn't work. They saw that they needed to deepen their relationship with them rather than turning them into a spiritual fixer-upper. Mel and Carol respect Nick and Jenny's journey, knowing that God is drawing them closer to each other and him through this challenging situation.

It's worth pointing out that having a desire for your kids to do something is different from having an agenda to make them do something. Nick and Jenny know where Mel and Carol stand. Mel and Carol haven't made a secret about hoping Nick and Jenny will share their Catholic faith. But Mel and Carol are willing to put that long-term desire on hold while they invest in the relationship, so that it's deep enough to handle the serious topics they would like to discuss.

Compare this approach to what would have happened if Mel and Carol had simply lectured Nick about leaving the Church or pressured him to get an annulment and have his second marriage recognized by the Church. What if Mel and Carol's passion for their Catholic faith had led them to pick fights around Sunday worship, religious practices, or holiday celebrations? Would that have drawn Nick and Jenny into a better relationship with Mel and Carol and the Church? Or would it have driven a wedge?

By taking a more respectful approach, Mel and Carol show that they are willing to leave their comfort zone so that the Holy Spirit can draw them into deeper communion with their adult son and daughter-in-law. God may indeed use Mel and Carol to call Nick and Jenny back to the Church, but in the meantime, God is giving them many opportunities for in-depth spiritual conversations. They are becoming more effective mentors to their son and daughter-in-law.

In this example, we used religion as the difficult topic, but the same process applies to other topics: politics, lifestyle choices, and so on. We have to meet our children where they are and lead them by walking beside them in whatever way we can.

In the parable of the lost sheep, the shepherd doesn't stay in the meadow yelling at the lost sheep to come back to join the flock. He goes off to find it. When he finds the sheep, he sets it on his shoulders and carries it home with great joy. The shepherd willingly leaves behind the comfort of the familiar in order to find and tenderly accompany the lost sheep (see Luke 15:1-7; Matthew 18:10-14).

We need to be willing to do the same. We allow God to work more effectively in us, through us, and with us when we find ways to meet our adult children where they are. This means that we acknowledge whatever good we can find in their choices while not pretending we're unconcerned about those choices, and then we use the stronger relationship as a springboard for deeper conversation.

FOR PRAYER

Lord, I ask you for the courage to love my children more than I love my comfort zone. Make me willing to see the good intentions behind my adult children's actions, even when I disagree about their positions and the approaches they take in pursuing their choices.

Help me be more like you, the faithful shepherd, so that I may be led by you and in turn lead my children closer to you in everything I say and do. Amen.

Holy Family, pray for us.

FOR REFLECTION

1. How does the approach outlined in this chapter either challenge or support the approach you have taken in conversations with your adult children?

2. Is there one small way in which you can do more to acknowledge the good intentions behind your adult children's beliefs or behaviors, even if you can't agree with those beliefs or behaviors?

3. What is one small step you could take to deepen your relationships with your adult children so that your relationships might be able to contain the conversations you wish to have?

CHAPTER FOUR

Understanding Influence

Why do we listen to some people but not to others? More specifically, why do our kids listen to other people and not to us? And what can we do about that?

The word "attachment" best describes why we're more open to the influence of some people while being closed to the influence of others. In most human relationships, it's not primarily a particular person's logical arguments or the force of their personality that convinces us to see things their way. Instead, attachment is at work.

"Attachment" describes the level to which a person has a gut-level sense that another person understands and cares for their heart. When we are attached to someone, we have an almost irresistible desire to share thoughts and feelings with them, seek their advice and counsel, and be open to their help.

We do this because, on an emotional level, we feel as if they "get" us and that it's safe to open up to them.

Please note, we're not saying that logic and charisma don't matter. It's just that they matter less than attachment. Without strong attachment, two people will be impervious to each other's reasoning or influence.

Although we like to think that attachment is automatic in certain relationships, such as the parent-child or the husband-wife relationship, that's not necessarily the case. Many spouses can say they have a good marriage because there is little conflict in the relationship, but they value the opinions of their friends more than the opinion of their spouse. Our heart naturally opens to the people to whom we feel attached.

Interestingly, attachment does not require that people agree with us. Disagreement won't typically undermine attachment, as long as we feel that the other person gets us and is willing to listen to us, affirming us where they can and framing their concerns in a way that helps us clarify our goals rather than putting up roadblocks.

What *does* undermine attachment is when a person perceives that the giver of advice is always a little too eager to get in the way or make it more difficult for them to pursue what they want in life.

Attachment Undermined

Jennifer, twenty-four, says that she would like to talk with her parents about some of the bigger life decisions she has to make. However, "They always act like the right answer is obvious to them and that if I don't agree right away, I'm an idiot. I know they mean well, but I wish they could help me figure things out for myself instead of telling me what to do. I need some space."

◆ ◆ ◆

Eric, thirty, knows that his parents wish that he and his wife would move closer to them so that they could be more involved in the lives of their grandchildren. Eric works remotely for his company, and so it would be possible. But, he says, "My parents are way too ready to share their opinions about everything. When we get together for the holidays, they constantly question how we parent, our rules—even our marriage relationship. They act as if they need to be hovering over us in order for my family to flourish.

"I love my folks, but if we lived closer, I'm not sure who'd be the first to kill the other. My parents bring up the move all the time, but I always change the subject as quickly as I can."

◆ ◆ ◆

In these two examples, Jennifer and Eric are willing to admit that their parents are good people and even have their best interests at heart. Unfortunately, their parents undermine attachment by putting more energy into asserting their opinions than in getting to know their children's hearts. In both cases, the parents' intentions are good, but their heavy-handed approach disrupts the attachment that could open their kids to their ideas.

Jennifer's and Eric's parents aren't abusive or unkind. But they presume they have a better relationship with their adult children than they actually have. As a result, they fall into the trap of pressing their agendas rather than taking the time to get to know their kids and their concerns.

If such a small thing can disrupt attachment, imagine how much more tension there would be in these relationships if they were complicated by divorce, abuse, addictions, or other traumatic events that negatively impact attachment between parents and kids. The wounds from those types of trauma will need to be healed—or the process of healing should at least be underway—before parents can have the important conversations they might want to initiate. In those more complicated cases, an experienced pastoral counselor can help parents navigate the sensitive territory and heal the wounds that prevent an adult child from trusting the parent, hearing the parent, or even allowing the parent to participate in their life.

Living in the Present

The fact is, attachment with adult kids can be relatively fragile. After all, it is the responsibility of adult kids to launch—to break attachment with their parents and rebuild it with their own spouse and children. Parents can't assume that any credits they earned from building attachment with their kids when they were little will carry over to adulthood. It's not that these efforts are lost altogether. It's that they tend to be relegated to the realm of pleasant memories.

The things that build attachment at one stage of a relationship don't necessarily carry over to the next stage. Parents can draw from these child- and teen-attachment experiences to earn the chance to build attachment with their adult kids, but that attachment still has to be built. It's easier to do this with some adult kids than others, for many reasons.

Parents must take time to get to know the unique goals, needs, concerns, hopes, and dreams of a particular adult child if they are to maintain attachment with that child. Then, through a process of supportive accompaniment, parents can open their adult child to the parents' concerns, hopes, and dreams. They can't guarantee that their adult children will do what they say, but they can increase the likelihood that their kids will truly hear them and respect and consider their opinions.

Part two of this book will look at different ways to plant the seeds of attachment, making it more likely that your adult children will be open to having conversations with you on subjects that are currently off-limits. For now, it's important to understand that the ability to have successful conversations—especially difficult conversations—with your adult kids depends less on specific communication skills or the history that you've shared than on making sure you are actively working to cultivate a relationship that is deep and strong enough to contain the discussions you want to have.

FOR PRAYER

Lord, give me the humility I need to see my adult children for who they are and my relationship with them for what it is. Give me the patience to meet them where they are; the ears to really listen to what they say; the heart to feel their concerns, hopes, ideas, and dreams; and the courage to work with them to heal what needs to be healed between us.

Teach me to respond to them in ways that open their hearts to mine, so that I can bring their hearts to you in every conversation we have. Amen.

Holy Family, pray for us.

FOR REFLECTION

1. What ideas in this chapter surprised or challenged your understanding of what it takes to have important and sometimes difficult conversations with your kids?

2. Have the ideas presented in this chapter challenged you to reevaluate the strength or depth of your relationships with your adult children? If so, in what ways?

3. We will offer specific tips for building attachment in part two of this book. But even now, can you think of some small things you could begin doing—or changes you could make—that would strengthen the attachment between you and your adult children?

CHAPTER FIVE

Response-ability

Charles called our radio program when we were discussing parents' relationships with their adult children. He said, "At what point do you just have to say, 'This is on my kids. I've done what I can'? My kids don't call or text me. I try to reach out to them, but they're always too busy. I'm tired of it, and I'm tired of feeling guilty about it. When can I stop blaming myself and just get on with my life?"

◆◆◆

When we discuss difficult relationships with adult children on our radio program, we inevitably get calls about blame. Raising kids is hard. We all do our best, and we all fear that we've failed in some way. As you've read through the first few chapters of this book, it's possible that you've felt you have either let your adult kids down or have come at conversations in a manner that made things worse.

This line of thought isn't helpful or productive, and we encourage readers to leave it behind. Blame—especially self-blame—accomplishes nothing and fosters anxiety, depression, and the feeling that we are stuck and powerless.

Self-blame is a kind of neurotic guilt that leaves us consumed with the problem in front of us without the energy to actually solve the problem. Healthy guilt allows us to recognize a problem and focus most of our energy on resolving it. Self-blame is a kind of unproductive guilt: we feel there's nothing we can ever do to address a bad situation and make it right.

Self-blame has a lot in common with scrupulosity, in that it blocks the grace of God that would allow us to address the problem. Both self-blame and scrupulosity produce feelings of powerlessness, isolation, and self-pity, none of which are among the gifts and fruits of the Holy Spirit.

Perhaps you came to this book feeling hopeless about your ability to heal your relationships with your adult kids. Or perhaps you've read something in the previous chapters that has stirred up the sort of scrupulous guilt that makes you want to give up. We urge you not to waste time dwelling in regret or futility.

Make a plan. If you don't know where to start, seek counsel. And get to work. The antidote to self-blame is *response-ability*.

In his book *Love and Responsibility*, Pope St John Paul II defines responsibility not as guilt, blame, or fault but as the *ability to respond* in the most loving way possible to any offense, wound, or problem.[2] When we allow ourselves to be flooded with bad feelings, such as unhealthy guilt, we end up reacting to situations in ways that are unproductive. Like Charles at the beginning of this chapter, we end up giving in to the hurt feelings and looking for someone to blame—ourselves or others—so that we can have an excuse to give up and walk away.

Whether your relationship with your adult child is simply not as deep as you wish, is strained, or is even nonexistent, the good news is that with God's grace, there is always something you can do to make it stronger, deeper, and healthier.

Persistence Pays Off

With God's grace, you have the ability to respond to any challenge that stands between you and the relationships you would like to have with your adult kids. In fact, we suggest that as a Christian parent whose job it is to model the loving, faithful accompaniment of God the Father (see *Catechism*, 239), you have an obligation to keep trying to build a healthier, deeper, and stronger relationship with each of your adult kids throughout your life.

Sometimes you will need to be humble enough to admit when you were wrong or when you committed some offense that—knowingly or not—damaged the relationship. Other times, you will need to reach out for the umpteenth time, knowing that you may not get the response you're looking for. Other times still, response-ability may require that you set certain limits or boundaries that irritate your adult child in the short term but open the door to a healthier relationship in the future.

Regardless, response-ability means that there is always something we can do to effect godly change in our life and relationships. If we prayerfully set our hearts and minds to the task of strengthening our relationships with our adult kids, we can count on God to multiply our efforts as he multiplied the loaves and the fishes (see Matthew 14:13-21).

It's good to acknowledge the problems that may be coming between you and your adult child, especially if you are responsible for some of those problems. It's important, however, that you avoid not only self-blame, hopelessness, and despair but also a desire to hurry up and solve it all so that you don't have to feel bad anymore. None of these attitudes are fruitful or godly.

In part two of this book, we'll look at ways you can begin building relationships big enough to contain the conversations you want to have. For now, it's enough to know that impulses to feel hopeless, to try to fix things, or to rush things are from the enemy, who wants you to remain estranged from your adult children. Resist those temptations, and focus on developing the ability to respond in love to your children, regardless of their situations. Focus on being supportive where you can be and building up the relationship wherever you can. Let the Holy Spirit guide you as you look for opportunities to make your relationships with your adult children big enough to contain the topics you want to discuss with them.

FOR PRAYER

Lord, help me resist the temptation to dwell on past mistakes or give in to feelings of self-blame or despair. Give me the grace to see my situation through eyes of hope. Help me acknowledge the problems that prevent my relationship with my adult child from being what I want it to be. Help me see these problems not as obstacles but as challenges to be overcome through your grace.

Help me develop the ability to respond in love to any barriers that come between me and my adult child. Make me receptive to the promptings of your Holy Spirit. Amen.

Holy Family, pray for us.

FOR REFLECTION

1. In your own words, how would you describe the difference between self-blame and response-ability?

2. How could cultivating the ability to respond in love to the challenges you face in your relationship lead you to approach your adult child differently than you have in the past?

3. Do you ever give in to feelings that say, "Nothing will ever change" or that make you rush to address big issues before your relationship is stable enough? What can you do in the future to avoid giving in to this temptation?

PART TWO

Planting the Seeds

We're now ready to explore how you can build relationships with your adult kids that are big enough to contain the conversations you want to have with them. We'll consider a basic framework for reaching out:

- how to become a more effective listener,
- how to unleash the power of forgiveness,
- how to support your adult child without endorsing choices you don't agree with, and
- making sure you don't undermine your credibility and create avoidable roadblocks to meaningful conversations.

CHAPTER SIX

Reaching Out: First Steps to Deeper Conversation

B y this point, we hope you understand that the reason you're struggling to have certain conversations with your adult kids is not that you don't have all the facts you need in order to challenge their opinions. Rather, for any number of reasons, your relationship is simply not deep or big enough. The good news? You have the ability to respond in a way that will build that strong relationship. This is true regardless of what caused the unhealthy or weak dynamic in the first place.

You may be asking, "But where do I begin?" In this chapter, we'll present a brief overview of the initial steps for building that relationship. In the remaining chapters of part two, we'll explore additional skills you'll need to make this template work for you.

To repeat, before we begin: the first step to cultivating a deeper relationship with an adult child is to bring that relationship to God. Not once. Not once in a while. Every day.

Likewise, don't ask God merely to change things for you. *Ask him to teach you what he wants you to do* to build the kind of relationships with your adult kids that will allow you to have any kind of conversation you feel you need to have. Specifically, ask God to help you learn how to respond to obstacles you face in a relationship in a manner that glorifies him and works for the ultimate good of you, your child, and your relationship.

Pray about this as if you were blindfolded and walking across a busy street guided only by your best friend. Think of God as that best friend. Let him use the challenges you face in your relationships with your adult kids to lead you and to draw you into closer communion with him.

Having grounded your efforts in prayer, the next step is to let relationships grow in as low-key a way as necessary, as we've discussed in previous chapters. Enjoy getting to know your kids; do whatever it takes to enlarge each relationship. When the time seems right, you can then tell your adult children that you would like to have stronger relationships with them. Don't make it a demand; make it an invitation. Say something like "I don't want to add anything else to your plate, but I'd love for us to be closer. It would mean a lot to me if you could let me know—or at least think about—ways that I could support you better or get a little more time with you doing something that you enjoy."

There is real humility in this request. You aren't saying, "You owe me a relationship, so pay up" or, even, "I want to be closer with you on my terms." It's "Help me understand how I can fit better into *your* life. Let me know what I can do to be a more supportive presence."

Recall what we said in chapter four about attachment. Having a securely attached relationship with someone means that they know—on a gut level—-that you are a person they can turn to for the support and guidance they need to live a fuller, richer, healthier, and happier life. Asking how you can better support them lets your adult kids know that you don't want to take up their time, complicate their lives, or give them "one more thing to do." Rather, this question shows that you are invested in them and that you want to invest in them even more.

Many adult children feel that their relationship with their parents is more an obligation than an actual relationship. The above question challenges that assumption. It implicitly says, "I don't want you to think of this relationship, on any level, as an obligation. I want you to look forward to seeing me and to feel supported when we spend time together."

Some readers might resist this at first. You are the parent, after all. Shouldn't your adult kids be more accommodating to you?

Not really. As parents, it's your job to find ways to continue to support their successful adulthood; it's not your job to guilt them into regularly paying tribute to their patriarch and matriarch. As Christian parents in particular, it's your job to disciple your kids into, and accompany them throughout, a successful, godly adulthood.

Sometimes supporting them in this manner will mean reaching out. Sometimes it will mean backing off. Other times, it will mean setting boundaries. The question of knowing *what* to do and when to do it is why we make prayer the foundation of our effort.

Regardless of whether we are reaching out, backing off, or setting boundaries, the goal is the same: At all times, we are not doing this in order to build ourselves up or make our adult kids feel they must be submissive to us. We are doing our best to work for their ultimate good in a manner that strengthens our relationships with them, allowing God to use us to bring our kids closer to him. The better we are at letting God show us which actions are best for particular circumstances, the stronger that relationship will become. We'll find that our kids will want to spend time with us, discuss their concerns with us, and be open to hearing our concerns and advice.

When you ask your kids, "How can I support you better?" they may be able to tell you, but often they may not have an answer. They may, at best, respond with "I don't know." That's when the next step comes in.

Don't just listen with your ears, but attend to what your children do in the days and weeks after you ask this question. Sometimes there will be a test. Your children may invite you to do something that they enjoy but you don't. They may bring up topics for discussion that have historically been difficult to deal with peacefully. They may ask for help at a time that is inconvenient for you.

Be on the lookout for these opportunities. They represent an effort on the part of your adult children to see if you really mean what you say. Do your best to be as generous as you can in responding to these invitations—because that's what they are.

Of course, you shouldn't approve of or participate in objectively immoral or degrading behavior, but do your best to be as generous as you can about invitations outside that category. The more accommodating you can be, the more likely it is that your adult children will see that you're serious about building a relationship that is large enough to contain the conversations you want to have with them.

Handling Challenging Requests

If your kids do ask you to show support for them by participating in something you believe is immoral or demeaning, you'll need to decline. But don't get defensive, and don't decline immediately. Instead, ask questions to try to understand what doing that thing means to them. For instance, you might say, "I know that's important to you, and I wish I could support you in all the ways you want me to. Can you help me understand what it would mean to you if I joined you in this?"

Notice, at no point in this response do you agree to do the thing that was asked of you. Neither do you decline to do it. You simply diffuse the bomb your child has thrown into the conversation by seeking more information. The answer to this question will help you explore other more acceptable ways to provide the benefit your child is seeking. Here's an example.

———— ◆ ◈ ◆ ————

Benita and Ron are the parents of Richard, a thirty-five-year-old man who identifies as homosexual. Both Benita and Ron love Richard very much, but their relationship with him has been strained over the years because of their concerns about his orientation and their objections to his sexually active lifestyle. There are many things they would like to discuss with Richard, but most of all, they wish he were more open to going to church and reconsidering his rejection of the Catholic faith in which they raised him.

In the short term, they have decided to let all of these issues go and focus instead on creating a strong relationship. Recently they asked Richard, "How can we do a better job of supporting you and fitting into your life?" In response, he challenged them to march with him in the city's upcoming gay pride parade. He told them that they owed it to him for all the years they have made him feel like a second-class citizen.

Benita and Ron had been clients in our telecounseling practice, and we had already discussed how this conversation might go. Although they didn't know exactly what Richard would ask, they knew, based on past experience, that he would probably counter with something they weren't ready or able to do. We had suggested saying, "We know that it hasn't always come across the way we want it to, but we love you so much. We really wish we could support you in all the ways you want to be supported by us. Can you help us understand what it would mean to you to have us walk with you?"

The point was not to imply that they would march in the parade. Benita and Ron were absolutely opposed to this for many reasons. Nevertheless, they really did want Richard to know that they wanted to love and support him in every way they could. That's why they asked the question.

The question challenged Richard to get beyond his defensiveness and really talk to them about what he wanted. He replied, "You guys have always made me feel like you're disgusted with me. Like I'm broken. And unless I can get with your agenda for my life, you really don't want anything to do with me. Not the real me anyway."

Understandably, this was hard for Benita and Ron to hear. There was a lot they disagreed with in his statement, and naturally they wanted to argue with him and counter him point for point. Because of our conversations, they resisted this.

Instead, they said, "Richard, we're so sorry that we've done anything that has ever made you feel that we were disgusted with you. Nothing could be further from the truth. We love you so much. We want the absolute best for you. It's true that means different things for us than it means for you, but we're not disgusted by you in the least. You are our son. You have so many gifts. And you are a blessing to so many people.

"We know we don't see eye-to-eye on a lot of really important things, but we promise that, even though we can't always do what you want, we want to do everything we can to show you how much we love you. We want to do a better job showing you all the ways we really are proud of you."

By using the question we proposed above, Benita and Ron were able to take Richard's emotionally volatile response and identify the deeper wound that needed to be addressed. They were able to avoid doing something they believed to be objectively immoral, but they were still able to identify ways they could do more to show Richard that they love him and are proud of many things about him. This exchange represented a huge step forward in their relationship and opened up many more avenues for future connection and communication. Obviously, there was still a long way to go in healing their relationship and getting to a comfortable place with each other, but this exchange represented a turning point in the cold war that had existed between them for years.

When parents take this approach, they can open doors that were previously bolted shut. Fortunately, not every conversation is so fraught with tension. But in any conversations you want to have with your adult children, this approach can give you a way forward.

You may be chomping at the bit to bring up the "big topic" (whatever it is), but restrain yourself for the time being. Your adult child will probably expect you to use the first few times together as an opportunity to bring up the hot-button discussion. If you do, they will be ready, and they will be defensive.

A good rule of thumb is to see them at least five times without discussing anything serious at all. It might take even longer—much longer—before you can ask if it would be OK to discuss X. If they say no, apologize gently for pushing—even if you don't feel that you were. Respect their boundary. Simply say that it is an important topic to you, that you'd like to discuss it sometime, but that you understand that the relationship isn't at a place where they are comfortable talking about it with you. Then do everything you can to make the rest of the time together as pleasant as possible.

You may feel that you're sweeping things under the rug. You are not. You're simply resisting the temptation to pour a gallon of water into a teacup, metaphorically speaking. Remember that the key to having successful conversations with your adult children is growing the relationships so that they are big enough to contain the conversations you want to have. This takes time, patience, and love.

The Gottman Relationship Institute is one of the most respected organizations in the United States to study relationship dynamics. The institute's research shows that in general, in order to deal effectively with difficult topics, people need to be in relationships that are twenty times more supportive, encouraging, affirming, loving, and kind than they are criticizing, complaining, or working through difficult things.[3] The lower the ratio between positive and negative exchanges, the more likely it is that the response will be defensive. When someone understands that the other person in the relationship is supporting them and is coming from a good place thirty-eight times out of forty, they are much more likely to extend the benefit of the doubt when difficult conversations arise.

The biggest part of building such a relationship is making sure that you are working to establish, reestablish, and maintain a positivity-to-negativity ratio that gets as close to the 20:1 ratio as humanly possible. This doesn't mean you have to agree with the other person or make grand gestures. Mostly it means putting in the time to be there, to show appropriate affection, to look for ways you can be affirming, to show interest and ask interesting questions, and to be seen as more helpful than antagonistic.

This always takes more effort than we think it will; for some parent–adult child relationships, it takes an immense amount of work. However, if you want to have free-flowing conversations—especially difficult conversations—with your adult children, this is the most important dynamic to establish.

When you experience pushback or resistance, don't attribute it to stubbornness on your adult child's part. Rather, attribute it to a downward shift in the positivity-negativity ratio, and address it. Developing this kind of sensitivity to the relationship dynamic is a big part of developing your capacity for response-ability.

Engaging in Conflict

In addition to research on relationship dynamics, there is another source of wisdom on how to have difficult conversations with your adult kids—one that might seem strange. Catholic just-war doctrine guides decisions on when it's appropriate to engage in conflict and how to go about it. Although the doctrine is written with armed conflict between nation states in mind, many elements apply to any conflict between two people or two groups of people.

One of the principles of a just war is that "there must be serious prospects of success" (*Catechism*, 2309). Otherwise you simply create more problems than you already have. The only way a conflict between two nations—or people—can be justified is if there is a reasonable chance that the outcome will be better than the current state of affairs. If that is not the case, the combatants must do what they can to avoid having a battle.

Here's how this principle can apply to your situation with your adult child. You may be experiencing a strong temptation to address a big issue the first chance you get—or every chance you get. In fact, you may feel a strong moral obligation to do so and incredible guilt if you don't. Imagine that in the middle of your emotional turmoil, your adult child responds to your efforts to build a relationship by giving you a chance to do something together. Immediately you think, "Aha! Finally we can have that talk I've been dying to have."

If you open your mouth at this stage, however, your adult child, feeling like a project rather than a person, will assume that you only spend time with them in order to browbeat them about the thing they really don't want to discuss with you. Their defenses will go up even higher, and you will probably need to wait ten or twenty times as long before you can bring up the topic again.

To sum up, the "wait until you've been together at least five times (or more) before bringing up the topic (or bringing it up again)" guideline isn't hard-and-fast. It's a rule of thumb. It's better to learn to read the room, so to speak. Do things seem comfortable and relaxed between you and your adult child? Have you had numerous successful, pleasant, and uneventful experiences together? Has your child begun inviting you, on their own, to do more things together or have more conversations of some depth? Have those conversations been going well?

If all these conditions exist, it's probably OK to ask if, at some point, you can broach the sensitive topic you want to discuss. Always keep in mind: if you want to have a successful conversation with your adult child, 90 percent of your focus should be on the strength and quality of the relationship before you bring up the topic, when you bring up the topic, while you are discussing the topic, and after you have left the conversation. Satan will try to use the conversation to drive a deeper wedge between you and your child. On the other hand, the Holy Spirit wants you to use the conversation to bring your adult child into deeper communion with you, allowing you to help bring that adult child into deeper communion with him. As St. Paul said,

> If I speak in human and angelic tongues but do not have
> love, I am a resounding gong or a clashing cymbal. And if I
> have the gift of prophecy and comprehend all mysteries and
> all knowledge; if I have all faith so as to move mountains
> but do not have love, I am nothing. (1 Corinthians 13:1-2)

You can always build on a pleasant superficial relationship, but you can't add to a house that's on fire. Focus your energies on praying for guidance and building up the relationship, putting in the time to be a part of your adult child's life in ways that feel supportive to them. If you do this, the Holy Spirit will give you opportunities to have those discussions you long to have.

FOR PRAYER

Lord, give me wisdom to respond to my adult child in a way that will always keep the strength, health, and vitality of our relationship in the forefront of my mind. Let me never be satisfied with simply saying words to my adult child so that I can congratulate myself on having "told them."

Rather, let me always know how to strengthen my relationship with my adult child through my attitude and through what I say and do.

Make me a good shepherd, as you are a good shepherd. Give me the grace to build the kind of relationship with my adult child that makes them want to open their heart to me, and then use me to help pour your heart into theirs. Amen.

Holy Family, pray for us.

FOR REFLECTION

1. How is the approach outlined in this chapter different from the approach you have been taking with your adult child?

2. What suggestions in this chapter seem to be the most likely steps you could take to strengthen your relationship with your adult child and start having more meaningful conversations?

3. In this chapter, we discussed Gottman's 20:1 positivity-to-negativity ratio. How would you describe the positive-to-negative ratio in your relationships with your adult children? What are a few things you could do to make gains in this area?

CHAPTER SEVEN

A Listening Heart

Give your servant, therefore, a listening heart. (1 Kings 3:9)

So it's finally happening. The Holy Spirit has given you an opportunity to discuss that topic you've been dying to address with your adult child. Now what?

In this chapter, we'll look at some basic strategies and techniques for having successful conversations. Successful conversationalists—especially those who deal with complicated topics—do twice as much listening as talking. They don't do this as a technique. They listen because they are genuinely interested in what the other person thinks, what motivates them, and what their goals, concerns, and needs are.

Successful conversationalists may not agree with everything that's being said, but they're careful not to rush to judgment. They ask questions. They show real care and concern. They look for points of agreement to build on. They don't try to change the person they're speaking with, but they do look for ways to be a positive influence while deepening the relationship.

Christians call this approach "accompaniment," a term often used in reference to building a discipleship relationship. Accompaniment is an active prayerful process that involves listening to another person, creating strong attachment with that person, and honoring their needs and concerns. When we operate in this dynamic, other people can become more open to receiving our guidance about how to meet their needs and address their concerns in godly ways.

"Accompaniment relationship" describes the best parent-and-adult-child relationships. We hope the following advice helps you learn how to have conversations with your adult child in a manner that facilitates a real accompaniment relationship.

Monitor and Manage Your Emotional Temperature

Managing your emotional temperature is the single most important technique you can learn if you want to have an effective conversation with anyone, especially an adult child. In fact, you will not be able to successfully use any of the information in this chapter, much less the rest of this book, if you don't actively work to master your emotional temperature first. Why?

To put it simply, for the purposes of this discussion, your brain is made up of three parts. Your "body brain" controls your bodily functions. Your "emotional brain" controls your emotional reactions and your fight, flight, or freeze response. Your "thinking brain" helps you learn new things and apply what you learn to new challenges. Everything you are learning in this book (and anywhere else, for that matter) is stored in your thinking brain.

There's a problem with all this.

When your emotional brain becomes overstimulated, your bloodstream floods with stress chemicals, which force your thinking brain to shut down. This is a deeply ingrained, primitive, and brain-based survival strategy. Basically, if you're being chased by a saber-toothed tiger, you don't want to have to think about it too much. You need to react. Unfortunately, the emotional brain is not very smart. It can't tell the difference between a saber-toothed tiger attack and your adult child yelling at you.

Your emotional brain doesn't really care what's going on outside of you. All it can do is recognize that the stress chemicals in your bloodstream are becoming elevated. If you let them get too high, your emotional brain initiates a strategy designed to conserve energy, react, and survive the experience you are going through. Mostly that means it literally turns off your thinking brain and engages your fight, flight, or freeze response.

Have you ever had the experience of watching yourself doing and saying things that you know you probably shouldn't do or say? Or maybe you shut down and couldn't think well enough to say anything. Maybe you started agreeing with the other person just to get them to stop talking. Maybe you lashed out in anger or started running off at the mouth with a completely unhelpful lecture.

When you see yourself responding in a way that you know isn't going to make things better and will probably make things worse, you may find yourself powerless to stop. You can criticize yourself afterward. You can feel guilty and regretful later, but you can't help yourself in the moment. What's worse is that, even when you promise that you'll do things differently the next time, you find yourself triggered and doing and saying the same unhelpful things over and over again. What's wrong with you?

Well, technically, nothing. Your brain is working exactly as it was designed to work in order to escape dangerous situations. The problem is that unless you consciously learn to identify—and manage—your stress temperature, you can accidentally trigger your emotional brain's threat response. This shuts down your thinking brain, blocking your ability to apply things you've learned, to learn from your mistakes, to do anything except fight your way through the situation. You run away from the conflict (literally or figuratively), shut down completely, or break into a lecture that shuts everyone else down.

Those are the only options for the emotional brain in the face of a perceived threat. They work adequately to get you out of a problem, but none of these strategies are able to effect any positive change whatsoever in terms of our topic—how to move a conversation forward. If you can't control the process by which your emotional brain overheats and leads you to shut down or lash out, you will be stuck in a cycle. You will find yourself doing the same things and expecting to get different results.

The good news is that anyone can learn to manage their stress temperature more effectively and respond—rather than react—in stressful situations (such as talking to adult kids about difficult issues). The first step is learning to be aware of your stress temperature, not just when you're dealing with a problem, but at all times. When you're aware of your stress temperature throughout the day and you work at managing it, you give your thinking brain the space it needs to assess and act, instead of yielding its power to the emotional brain.

Take a look at the following chart. Pay particular attention to the behavioral signs that show your stress temperature rising. Those signs are key to the process.

People tend to underestimate how high their stress temperature is. They assume that unless they're throwing a tantrum, they're under control. That's not the case. Most people are incapable of engaging in effective, meaningful conversations—especially difficult conversations—unless they know how to keep their temperature at a six or lower.

The problem is, most people don't even attempt to engage in a difficult conversation until they are at a seven or beyond. That's because no one wants to have difficult conversations, so we ignore things until we can't anymore. And the reason we can't is because we're too drunk on our neurochemistry to care if we blow everything up.

At a six or lower, you can initiate a difficult conversation—not because you can't hold back anymore, but because, out of love, you need to address a serious concern. You're trying to find a solution that will work for everyone involved. Clearly, this is a different approach to conversations than most people take.

Here's a rule of thumb: the more difficult the conversation you wish to have with your adult child, the more you need to do to take down your emotional temperature first, and the

Stress Temperature/Behavioral Signs

1-3	Relaxed, focused, engaged, and fully able to respond rather than react to challenges.
4-5	A little less relaxed but still in control of self. You find it relatively easy to be respectful, pleasant, and solution oriented (instead of frustrated, irritable, and blame focused), even when you're experiencing a problem or facing a challenge.
6	Your bloodstream is flooding with stress chemicals. You can still be respectful, pleasant, and solution focused, but you are having to work at it. People are noticing that you seem stressed. They might ask, "Are you OK?" to which you respond, "What do you mean? I'm FINE."
Thinking Brain "Buffering"	
7	You begin to get "buzzed" on the stress chemicals flooding your bloodstream. The nonverbal filters in your thinking brain are starting to go offline. You begin to act frustrated and not care who notices. You might grimace, huff and puff, or make disgusted noises that indicate "I can't believe I have to deal with this." You're frowning, and you're fidgety. All these behaviors are meant to say to people, "You're stressing me out! Proceed with caution!"

Stress Temperature/Behavioral Signs

	Emotional Brain Now in Control
8	The verbal filters in your brain are collapsing. You aren't yelling or calling names, but you are beginning to either (1) agree with people (or say "whatever"), just to make them stop talking; (2) blame and deflect or make excuses; or (3) lecture and "helpfully" explain why it's entirely the other person's fault and how they'd better get their act together. You have lost your ability to empathize or listen.
9	Verbal filters have collapsed. Either you are completely shut down and unable to speak, or you are lashing out in anger and frustration. The goal is not so much to solve the problem as it is to let the other person know how horribly they are behaving and what a source of pain they are to you.
10	Your moral filters have collapsed. You are now doing and saying things that you would never say or do if you were emotionally sober. You may not even remember what you said or did when you calm down. When other people try to remind you, you will most likely deny it because you were "black-out drunk" on your stress chemicals.

harder you have to work to manage that temperature during the conversation.

Strategies for Lowering Your Emotional Temperature

Our book *Unworried: A Life Without Anxiety* offers an extensive look at strategies for lowering your emotional temperature. Although that book is about managing stress, worry, and anxiety, the process is the same for learning to manage your emotional temperature, regardless of the particular emotions involved. Here are a few simple techniques you can use to take down your emotional temperature before and during a difficult conversation with your adult child.

Pray

Ask God to help you remember that your adult child is not intentionally being difficult but, rather, is struggling. Ask God for ears to hear what their struggle is, for compassion and patience if and when they lash out in their pain, and for the wisdom to know how to respond in a manner that will bring out the best in them.

Slow Down

One of the first behavioral signs that we are approaching a seven is that we start to speak and act more quickly and unthinkingly. We start to trip over our words and make stupid mistakes, such as knocking over the glass we're reaching for. This is because the emotional brain doesn't care about any of that. It just wants to get us out of the perceived danger.

To lower your stress temperature, one deceptively simple technique is to deliberately slow down. Speak a little more slowly than you want to. Instead of thinking of all the things you have to do next, focus your mind on what you're doing now. If you're walking, pay attention to where you're putting your feet. Look at the coffee cup when you're reaching for it.

Slow down. This forces your thinking brain to stay online by making it do what it does best: focus and plan.

Pray with Your Adult Child

If things start to heat up in a conversation with your adult child, interrupt the conversation by saying, "I'm sorry. I just need a minute." Then, if they're open to it (and sometimes even if they're not), launch into some version of the following brief prayer: "Lord, I know what I want. And [name] knows what they want. Help us figure out what you want for both of us and how to take care of each other while we figure it out. Please let us remember how much we love each other, and help us use this situation to draw closer to you and each other. Amen."

Even most adult children who would prefer not to pray will find little to object to in this prayer. At worst they will roll their eyes at your religious affectation. In most cases, as long as the participants' stress temperatures are seven or lower, this strategy is particularly effective. Any higher temperature, and it may not work as well.

Take Care

No matter how much your brain wants you to think of your adult child as the problem, fight the temptation with all your might. Look for ways to get them to partner with you in solving the problem, whatever it is. Many of the techniques that follow in this chapter will help you with this.

For now, it's enough to look for little ways to encourage each other through the tension and toward solutions. Say things like "I'm sorry this is so hard. I really do love you" or "Thank you for being willing to talk through this with me" or "I really appreciate your being willing to talk about this even though it's difficult" or "I know I'm frustrating you, but I really do want what's best for you. I'm sorry if that isn't coming across."

Statements like these will help you remember that it's your job, as the more mature adult, to shepherd your child through the tension and toward solutions. These statements will also make it hard for your adult child to cast you in the role of enemy combatant.

Take Little Breaks

When all else fails, take a short break. Not the kind where you say, "I can't talk about this anymore!" and storm off. (That's what happens at a nine or ten temperature reading.) We're talking about short breaks, when you excuse yourself to use the restroom (whether you need to or not) or get a drink (and offer to get them something while you're at it).

When you're out of the room, check the thoughts going through your head. Are they telling you that you raised an idiot and that you wish you could disown them?

Force yourself to see the situation through their eyes—not to agree with them or excuse any frustrating behavior, but so that you can empathize with them and begin to see what they're trying to accomplish by believing, acting, or speaking as they do. If you do this properly, when you come back to rejoin the conversation, you should be able to

- have either a sense of the good intention behind their actions or a willingness to hear more about it or
- have a question in mind to move the conversation forward.

An example of the latter might be someting like "I know this is hard, but thanks for being willing to talk it through with me. Even though we don't see eye-to-eye, can you help me know what I can do to show you that I really am on your side and want the best for you?"

When you do these things, you're practicing caretaking in conflict, a critical skill that enables two people to keep their stress temperatures down by reminding them that they are not enemies. Rather, they are two people who love each other, want the best for each other (even if it doesn't feel like it in the moment), and want to do their best to work things out. These messages help the emotional brain calm down and trust the thinking brain to use its tools, strategies, and wisdom to find effective solutions.

If you find that just thinking about talking through something with your adult child causes your stress temperature to rise to an eight or higher, and you are unsuccessful in bringing it down, consider seeking help from a professional pastoral counselor.

Moving the Conversation Forward

You don't have to have your emotional temperature mastered in order for the other suggestions in this chapter (and this book in general) to work. You just have to be intentional about learning to manage it. Then you can use the techniques that follow to move the conversation forward as you keep an eye on your internal temperature.

Don't Lecture

Too often we're so excited to finally have the chance to discuss something that we dump all our thoughts on the other person at once. Recall that this book uses the metaphor of tending a garden as the basis for understanding how to have meaningful and sometimes difficult conversations with our adult kids. With that in mind, lecturing is akin to overfertilizing and overwatering. It's an information dump that stifles real conversations and ultimately suffocates relationships.

How do you know if you're prone to lecturing?

- You find yourself in a monologue. You often speak for three or more minutes without asking a question or seeking any kind of input from others.
- You're more passionate about certain topics than you are about the people with whom you're discussing those topics.

- You have a hard time "reading the room." You often find yourself pouring out your heart, only to be surprised when the people you're speaking to either passive-aggressively resist or are openly hostile to you or your ideas. You're often hurt by this but have no idea why it happens. (Hint: it happens because you talk more than you listen.)

People who lecture mean well, but that doesn't change the fact that the road to hell is paved with good intentions. Lecturing does little more than make you feel good for having "told them" without actually allowing you to have any appreciable impact on another person's life, beliefs, or behavior. If you feel tempted to lecture, ask God to give you the grace to close your mouth and open your ears.

Use Soft Opens

Good communicators use soft opens instead of hard opens. An "open" refers to the way you start a conversation. A soft open is friendly, helpful, clear, nonjudgmental, solution focused, open-ended, and inviting. A hard open is hostile or critical, too broad, unfocused, loaded with emotional baggage, problem centered, closed, and stifling.

For example, let's say you want to talk about the way your adult child handles her money.

Soft Open: "I remember how hard it was for me to learn to keep to a budget. It can be one of the hardest parts of 'adulting.' Do you ever feel overwhelmed trying to come up with a budget or stick to one?"

Hard Open: "I can't believe you have so much on your credit cards! You're going to be paying that down for the rest of your life. You need to be way more responsible than that. What's wrong with you? You need to make a plan to get control of your finances, or you're really going to be in a mess."

The difference is obvious. People who primarily use hard opens often object to the soft-open approach. They feel that it tiptoes around the problem. But while soft opens may tiptoe *up to* a sensitive topic, they don't tiptoe *around* it.

A person who uses a hard open believes they won't get another chance to say what they need to say, so they better get it all out at once. Of course, the importance of their message then gets lost in a sea of hurt feelings. People who habitually use hard opens usually experience terrible results, but they comfort themselves by saying, "Well, I told them!" Telling someone something is not the same as accompanying and discipling. Telling is self-serving. Accompanying is other-centered.

By contrast, people who use a soft open are confident in their ability to feel out the best time and the best way to have a conversation. They don't feel the need to dump everything at once. They're comfortable playing a long game and confident that, in time, they have the skills to get where they need to go. The soft open is just that: an opening.

But what if the adult child in this example denies having a problem with money? That leads to the next tip.

Complain, Don't Criticize

A complaint describes a fact and asks for input. It gives you a gentle way to push back at initial resistance when you try to address a topic. A criticism makes an accusation and expects capitulation, but it usually gets a defensive response. Let's imagine the next step in that parent's attempt to address their adult child's money-management skills.

Parent: "I remember how hard it was for me to learn to keep to a budget. It can be one of the hardest parts of 'adulting.' Do you ever feel overwhelmed trying to come up with a budget or stick to one?"

Adult Child: "I don't know. I don't worry about it too much. I think I'm doing OK."

Parent, responding in criticism mode: "I'm glad you feel that way, but I guess I don't know how to square that with what you were telling me last week about your credit card balances. It sounded as if you were pretty concerned. If you'd be willing, I'd like to help you review your options and figure out the best way forward so that you don't get in over your head. Could we work on it together?"

This might not sound like any "complaint" you've heard before. That's understandable. This is a very specific way to complain about something. Again, for our purposes, a complaint describes a problem and asks for input. It can even offer some initial thoughts about how the problem could be addressed, although it tends to leave this at least a bit open-ended. A complaint tries to build a partnership around both the problem and the search for possible solutions. "I think we're both concerned about this. I'd like us to work together to figure it out."

Compare this to how a criticism would play out in the same exchange.

Parent: "I remember how hard it was for me to learn to keep to a budget. It can be one of the hardest parts of 'adulting.' Do you ever feel overwhelmed trying to come up with a budget or stick to one?"

Adult Child: "I don't know. I don't worry about it too much. I think I'm doing OK."

Parent, responding in criticism mode: "There you go again, living in some fantasy world where everything is going to fix itself. I don't understand how you can be so irresponsible! You need to get your spending under control, or you're really going to be sorry."

Again, the criticism is well-intended and perfectly understandable. Any parent would be concerned about their adult child's mounting debt. But approaching the issue by criticizing the adult child will only have the effect of shutting down the conversation and making it harder to bring the topic up another time.

Even if the adult child in our first example refuses to address the complaint, the parent has spent very little emotional capital. The parent using the complaint strategy can easily return to the issue after having several more positive contacts with the adult child. Meanwhile the parent employing the criticism-based approach, in the second example, may not even get another opportunity to connect with the adult child in the near future, much less another chance to raise this hot-button issue. Not only will the parent be unable to help the adult child handle their finances, but their relationship might end up defined by, or revolving almost entirely around, this contentious issue.

Diffuse

No matter how deft a conversationalist you are, conversations about difficult topics will inevitably escalate. This doesn't mean that you're doing something wrong. Don't be intimidated when temperatures rise.

How you respond to the escalation can spell the difference between an effective conversation and a failed attempt. If you respond by becoming more argumentative, defensive, or hostile, or if you are bent on proving that the other person has it all wrong, you're pouring verbal fuel on an emotional fire.

Arguments don't escalate because the other person fails to understand you. Arguments escalate because the other person is afraid you don't care about them—or at least, that you care more about your agenda than you do about them. So what do you do instead? Remember that *escalation is an invitation to affirmation.*

This can be challenging because the last thing you want to do when you're frustrated with someone is to affirm them. However, affirming someone doesn't mean agreeing with them or accepting disrespectful behavior. It means responding in a way that says, "Despite our differences, I am here for you. You can count on me. I love you."

No matter how frustrated we are with our adult children, we want them to feel that we're on their side and want the best for them.

Follow these steps if you want to effectively affirm someone and diffuse a situation:

1. Don't respond to the content of what they say.
2. Instead, empathize with the emotion behind the content.
3. Redirect toward solutions.

In our discussion about money management, the conversation could unfold like this:

Adult Child: "There you go again. No matter what I do, I can never be good enough. There's always something else I'm doing wrong."

Parent:
Step 1. Doesn't respond to the content or become defensive.
Step 2. Practices empathy. "I'm sorry that you feel so criticized by me. It's not what I'm trying to do, but I get that it feels that way. That makes me sad."
Step 3. Redirects. "Take me out of the picture for a second. If I weren't here pushing you to deal with this, how would you handle it? Do you feel you have some good solutions? Help me understand your plan."

In this example, the parent didn't have to agree with what the child said or defend himself in order to affirm the child. All the parent did was empathize with the emotion and try to redirect the adult child to begin thinking about solutions.

This approach works whether you are dealing with a tangible topic, like money management or parenting, or an intangible topic like religion or values. In the following situation, the adult child hasn't been going to church and tends to be defensive anytime the topic of religion comes up.

Adult Child: "Look, I believe in God, but church doesn't mean anything to me. I'm tired of having you rub this religion stuff in my face all the time."

Parent:
Step 1. Doesn't respond to the content or become defensive.
Step 2. Practices empathy. "It stinks to feel as if you're being judged by your parent and being forced to think in certain ways or do things you don't believe in anymore. It really isn't what I'm trying to do, but I get that you feel that way."
Step 3. Redirects. "You say that you believe in God, and I believe you. But could you help me understand how that belief makes a difference in your daily life? For me, going to church is one way that I say that God is making a difference in my life. Like, he matters enough that I make time to spend with him. I understand you're in a different place, but help me understand what your belief in God means to you and what difference it makes in your life."

The parent in this example is able to avoid an escalation while still gently challenging the adult child to consider how God is part of their daily life—and how he might be an even greater part. Although that may not be as satisfying as simply getting the adult child to go to church, it's certainly a step in the right direction. It can lead to conversations in which the parent and adult child can talk about how God is showing up for them and how they are responding to his presence.

Some readers might be chomping at the bit to see how these conversations end. How do you successfully get from Point A, where your adult children don't agree with you, to Point B, where they are willing to consider what you say, or maybe even to Point C, where they agree with you? If that's your reaction, let us gently challenge you to see that you're missing the larger point. Namely, there is no A-B-C solution to overcoming disagreements with anyone. It's messier than that. The techniques we're giving you will help improve your relationship and move the conversation along, but they probably won't result in a one-and-done discussion in which you work out all your differences.

What the techniques will do is help you make your relationship deep enough to contain the conversation you want to have and keep it going over time, until you can come to a better place. As long as the relationship is growing—even a little bit—and as long as the conversation is still in play, God can use the pathways you've built to open hearts and maybe change minds. But without that relationship and without an ongoing conversation about a difficult topic, you're going to need a miracle to see any real change.

The good news? While you may (and should) pray for miracles, you don't have to feel trapped until you get one. You can still cooperate with God's grace to diffuse the tension when difficult topics come up and actively work to move the conversation forward in productive directions.

In sum, don't view resistance, antagonism, or other forms of escalation as an indication that you simply need better facts to counter their facts or that you need to do a better job defending yourself or that you need more effective strategies for overcoming their obstinancy. Instead, realize that an *escalation is an invitation to affirmation,* and respond accordingly. If you do, you'll be able to use every moment in your conversations with your adult kids, even the difficult moments, as opportunities to grow closer to each other and understand each other better.

Asking Clarifying Questions

Conversation often breaks down when the person we're speaking with says something that doesn't make sense to us, seems absurd to us, or makes us feel attacked, judged, or misunderstood. The diffusing techniques we have recommended so far can work when the person we're speaking with feels that *we* don't care about *them.* Asking clarifying questions, on the other hand, works well when we're not so sure *they* care about *us.*

When we feel attacked, judged, or misunderstood, our natural tendency is to react—to defend ourselves. We assume that the other person *intends* to be offensive. But even when a person seems antagonistic, we can't know their true intentions. And so charity and good psychology should prevent us from reacting harshly. Instead, we can choose to be humble and give the other person the benefit of the doubt.

That doesn't mean that we let people—especially our adult kids—walk all over us. It means that the best way to challenge what they're saying to us, or the way they are saying it, is to ask a question that clarifies whether their words and behavior match their intentions.

Clarifying questions don't accuse or challenge. They hold up a mirror and say, "Is this really the look you're going for?" Here are some examples of clarifying questions:

- It seems as if you're not only saying you don't want to talk about this but also saying you don't want to deal with it. I understand that this is a tough topic, but is that really what you're trying to say?
- When you looked at me like that, I felt as if you think I'm an idiot. Is that how you feel about me?
- Whenever we talk about this, something about your tone makes me feel that you think I'm your enemy. Do you really feel that way?
- Something about the way you're talking to me makes me feel that you wish I would go away and leave you alone. Is that how you feel?
- When you said that, it sounded as if you were saying you resent almost everything about the way I raised you. Is that really what you're trying to say?

There are three steps involved in asking clarifying questions. You can use this basic format to address almost any behavior:

- Identify the specific behavior (what was said or done).
- Communicate the message you received from what was said or done.
- Ask if you understood the intended message correctly.

For this technique to work, you have to assume that the other person did not intend to be hostile; rather, there has been a miscommunication or a misunderstanding. Assuming this may sometimes seem foolish. For instance, if your adult child cusses you out, what possible intention could they have but to hurt your feelings?

You'd be surprised. In such a situation, ask a clarifying question. Instead of saying, "How dare you talk to me like that!" say, "When you talk to me like that, I feel that you're saying you hate me. Is that what you really mean?"

The first statement would probably result in an escalation. The second will more likely result in the clarification that your adult child doesn't, in fact, hate you; they're just hurt, scared, or overwhelmed. That doesn't justify their behavior, but it does give you a safe way to address it. If they admit that they are hurt, scared, or overwhelmed and that they are taking it out on you, you will then have the opportunity to be gracious and help them through it.

Clarifying a situation in this way allows you to practice the art of charitable interpretation. To put it another way, it allows you to "bear wrongs patiently," a spiritual work of mercy. Charitable interpretation doesn't make excuses for bad behavior or avoid addressing it. What it does, ultimately, is acknowledge that, given the chance, the offender will be willing to work through the problem with you.

Clarifying questions make the art of charitable interpretation possible. At the same time, they allow you to challenge irrational thinking and antagonistic or confusing behavior in a manner that is gentle, effective, and respectful. This opens the door to deeper understanding for all who are part of the discussion.

Solution-Focused Thinking

Conversations also break down over the idea that everyone has to agree on what happened before they can solve a problem: Who said what to whom? Who started it? What *actually* happened?

The truth is, it's extremely rare for two people to agree on any of this. Even people in great relationships, who generally see eye-to-eye on most things, will have very different interpretations of offenses. Many people spend years arguing about what actually happened, sinking into deeper despair about finding answers because they can't even agree on the problem.

As you might imagine, this is a huge issue in marital counseling, but the challenge applies to relationships of all types, especially relationships between parents and adult children. The answer is to avoid the problem altogether by using solution-focused thinking and solution-focused questions.

In a solution-focused approach, two people don't have to agree on what happened. They only need to agree that they both don't like what happened and don't want it to happen again. Regardless of who started it or who said or did what to whom, they can focus their energy on how to handle similar situations the next time.

Here's an example of how this might work, taken from a session Greg had with a mother and daughter about a contentious family issue:

◆◆◆

Jennifer was deeply hurt. She and her sister, Barb, disagreed about how to handle the holidays after their mother passed away. The real issue, however, was that Jennifer felt that her daughter, Emily, took her Aunt Barb's side in the family dispute. No matter how often Jennifer and Emily tried to discuss the situation, things got worse because they could never agree on what really happened. Jennifer accused her daughter of lying to cover up her "betrayal," and Emily accused her mother of starting the whole thing by acting like a child. Both became angrier and more estranged as the weeks went by.

As we discussed the drama in a session of family therapy, I suggested that, even if they couldn't agree on what happened, they could probably agree that neither of them were happy with the way things played out. Reluctantly, though they were both still hurting, they agreed this was the case.

I suggested that since they agreed on this point, it might be better to focus our energies on how to handle similar situations in which Barb might try to come between them. I asked them to think of rules they might keep in mind when negotiating conversations among the three of them. After some thought, Emily said there were two things she wished she'd done.

First, she wished she hadn't tried to make peace or run interference between her mom and her aunt. In the future, she would simply insist they talk directly to one another rather than enter into their disagreements. Second, she promised to offer her own opinion about issues and asked that Jennifer respect her opinion and not see it as an attempt to take sides or alienate her.

For her part, Jennifer said she'd take any comment Barb made about what Emily told her with a big grain of salt. Further, she'd check any such comments with Emily before reacting to them. She also agreed that it was unfair to put Emily in the middle of a dispute between Jennifer and her sister. If she had a complaint about Barb, she'd take it to Barb.

Both Jennifer and Emily agreed that, had these rules been in place earlier, they would probably have avoided the conflict that led them to counseling. They agreed that moving forward, things would go better if they stuck to these new rules for managing their relationship with each other and with Barb. Jennifer and Emily never did agree on what happened, but they felt good about their ability to navigate similar situations in the future. This allowed them to move on—together.

A solution-focused approach involves the following:

1. Even if you can't agree on anything else, agree that everyone involved could have done a better job handling the situation that triggered the disagreement.

2. Stay focused on this question: "What do each of us need to do in order to handle similar situations more effectively in the future?"

3. As much as possible, focus on what you personally could do better should similar situations arise. Don't tell other

people what they should do differently. The goal is to reflect on what each party could do to make similar situations go better in the future.

A few other points: Sometimes people get caught up in the idea that nothing like this will ever happen again, and so there's no need to work out an approach in case of future disagreements. For instance, if Jennifer and Emily were arguing over funeral arrangments for Jennifer's mother, they might think, "Well, Grandma isn't going to have another funeral." But it doesn't have to be the exact same circumstance. There will probably be other emotionally loaded family events that require planning and involve a high risk of conflict. How will you handle *those* situations?

Also, there are some limitations to this approach. You can take a solution-focused approach to 90 percent of personal problems, but in situations in which one person perpetrated violence against another or the family of origin is characterized by a persistently hostile environment—for example, high conflict, physical or sexual abuse, neglect, drug and alcohol abuse, and so on—it isn't enough to agree to disagree on what happened and focus on the future. Yes, even in these situations, you can have solution-focused conversations about how to be safe in each other's presence or how to handle day-to-day interactions, but for such serious issues, the offender must be willing to acknowledge and seek forgiveness for the damage they have done. Only then can true reconciliation occur.

If problems like these are at the root of the tension between you and your adult child, you need to deal with them directly and courageously. You may also need professional help in order to develop the skills needed to handle such delicate and emotionally charged issues. Forgiveness and reconciliation are possible in such situations, but you cannot gloss over the underlying problems. See the following chapter for more on this topic.

Such serious issues aside, solution-focused thinking can help parents and adult children negotiate a host of hot-button topics. Remember, don't worry that you can't agree on what happened, who started it, and who said what to whom. Agree that none of you are happy with the way the situation played out. Work together as a team to decide how you will handle future situations so that all of you feel cared for, appreciated, and understood.

The techniques in this chapter will increase the likelihood that conversations with your adult children are pleasant and productive. Remember, though, that it is always best to take the long view, especially if you're discussing difficult or highly emotional topics. Don't ever assume you'll resolve an issue in one conversation, and don't be discouraged if a discussion goes badly. Focus on building the relationship and learning from missteps. Then reengage when it seems that the relationship is deep enough to contain the conversation you need to have.

The more you are willing to see conversations with your adult children as a process rather than an event, the more likely you will be to discover healthy ways to engage in any discussions you would like to have with them.

FOR PRAYER

Lord, in my conversations with my adult children, help me communicate that I am on their side, even when we don't see eye-to-eye. Help me respond rather than react to the things they say that irritate me or that I do not agree with. Give me the grace to be a good listener and to take the lead in seeking solutions with my adult children. Amen.

Holy Family, pray for us.

FOR REFLECTION

1. Which of the techniques in this chapter would be the most useful in helping you have more meaningful conversations with your adult children?

2. Which of the techniques in this chapter would be the most difficult for you? What can you do to become more comfortable using them?

3. How does the solution-focused approach to conversation differ from your usual approach? How can you use this new approach in conversations with your adult children?

CHAPTER EIGHT

Seeking Forgiveness

Deborah is the mother of Alexa, a thirty-four-year-old mother of three. Deborah and her daughter have always had a challenging relationship, but things have gotten worse lately. Alexa is frustrated with Deborah over what she perceives to be Deborah's criticism of her children and her parenting abilities. To suggest that their last conversation on the topic was a disaster would be putting it mildly. Deborah, in particular, left the discussion feeling terribly hurt by the way Alexa treated her.

Deborah said, "I understand if she doesn't want me to comment on her parenting style. It's hard for me to not say things, but I get it. They're her kids. It's her job. I thought it would be OK to ask a few questions about her decisions without upsetting the apple cart, but I guess not. I'm actually OK with her telling me to butt out. But she was so cold the last time we talked. She insulted me a million ways to Sunday and then hung up on me. We didn't talk for several days after that.

"To be honest, I was happy to get the space. But then suddenly she texts me out of the blue as if nothing ever happened. I don't want to hold anything over her head, and I certainly don't want to jeopardize the relationship, but I can't get past how she treated me. Frankly, I don't trust her not to do it again. I'm not sure how to move forward. I feel like I deserve an apology. But I don't know how to approach that without blowing everything up again."

◆ ◆ ◆

Maddie is the thirty-four-year-old unmarried daughter of Connie and Martin, who divorced when Maddie was twelve. Martin had had an affair, the divorce was ugly, and Maddie never got along with Martin's new wife, Bethany. Connie eventually remarried, and Maddie had a decent relationship with her stepdad, but they were never close.

Maddie is successful in her career but has always been uneasy about relationships, largely because of her experiences growing up. The constant tension between Connie and Martin—often over her—crushed her spirit and made her feel that she couldn't count on having a healthy relationship of her own. Maddie is in counseling and making good progress, but her parents make a regular point of pushing her to date, telling her that she's too picky, and challenging her about why she feels the need to be in counseling.

As Maddie explains it, "They know that I'm doing therapy largely because of the impact their divorce had on me and on my own romantic relationships. The thing is, they both *want to deal with it by telling me to get over it. Especially my dad. 'C'mon Maddie,' he says to me. 'It was twenty-two years ago. You need to move on and live your life.' I know he means well, but I sometimes want to punch him when he says stuff like that. My mom does a little better at trying to empathize, but sometimes she gets frustrated too and accuses me of trying to put a guilt trip on them, blaming them for my problems.*

"*I don't blame them. I actually love them both very much. But it would really help if they could tell me that they're sorry for what happened and for how their choices hurt me. That they got it. I just don't ever feel they take me seriously.*

"*Sometimes they get upset that I don't visit more—especially over the holidays—but it's too emotionally exhausting. Not just because it brings up a lot of stuff for me, but also because I feel I have to keep my guard up all the time. If I say anything that makes them uncomfortable, they turn it back on me.*

"*I wish they'd be willing to see how their attitude hurts me and apologize. It wouldn't fix everything, but it would make it a lot easier to spend time with them.*"

◆ ◈ ◆

It's often necessary, when discussing important or difficult topics, to seek or extend forgiveness. This could be because of something we said or did in the course of a conversation or something someone said or did to us. Other times the conversation itself revolves around the need for forgiveness for a past hurt or offense that has festered and damaged the relationship, such as in the examples above.

Whether these kinds of hurts are the obstacles preventing you from having meaningful conversations with your adult kids or healing these hurts is the point of the difficult conversations you want to have, it's important to know how to navigate the challenges to forgiveness.

Asking for an Apology

If you have been hurt, you have the right to ask for an apology. Period. In the words of Pope St. Gregory the Great, "Thoughts seethe all the more when corralled by the violent guard of an indiscreet silence."[4] In other words, you can't achieve peace with another person by keeping everything inside. You have a right to ask for an apology if you have been hurt, and you have an obligation to seek forgiveness if you hurt the other.

It's important to know how to ask for an apology, however. Everything we discussed about soft opens and criticisms vs. complaints applies doubly in this case. Here are some examples of how the protagonists in the stories above should not and should approach asking for an apology.

DON'T
Deborah to Alexa: "I don't understand why you have to be so touchy when we talk about parenting. It's fine with me if you don't want to discuss it, but you owe me an apology for the way you treated me last time."

Maddie to her parents: "You guys are always pushing me to date and have relationships, but you're never willing to admit what you did that makes it hard for me to trust anyone I date—or even myself—to make something work. You just want me to get over it so you can stop feeling guilty. You're never really sorry for what you did."

While the feelings behind these statements are real, it's hard to imagine that Deborah or Maddie will get anything but a defensive response. Although what they say is heartfelt and honest, it's also antagonistic, blaming, and problem focused. In short, these are hard opens and criticisms.

DO

Deborah to Alexa: "Obviously, I crossed a line when I asked you about your parenting choices. I didn't mean to come off as critical. I'm so sorry. It hurt my feelings when you said what you said and then hung up on me.

"Although I never intend to, I'm probably going to step on your toes now and again. It would mean a lot to me if we could figure out a better way to handle those times when you feel I'm overstepping my bounds. Would you be willing to work on that with me?"

Maddie to her parents: "I don't mean to make you uncomfortable, and I promise you I'm doing everything I can to find someone to build my life with. But part of my problem is that I'm afraid of not being heard, of not being taken seriously. And part of that is because every time I try to talk about how your choices hurt me growing up, I feel like you blow me off and tell me to get over it.

"I'm doing my best to do that. But it would mean a lot to me if I felt that you understood how hard it was for me to grow up that way. I don't want to blame you for anything. I know it's hard for you, and I love you very much, but I want to know that you think my feelings are valid and that you're sorry for your part in all this."

These are examples of soft opens and complaints. Recall that a complaint describes the problem but focuses on getting a buy-in from the other person to find a solution together. It's likely that complaints like these would get a more supportive, empathic response than criticisms would. Note that in this "DO" version, both Deborah and Maddie were completely honest about what hurt them, but they framed their requests for an apology in a manner that focused on what they needed.

Asking for an apology this way doesn't come easily. It takes thought, reflection, and preparation. But it's worth it.

Think through what you want an apology to accomplish. Write out what you want to say. How you frame your request can make the difference between a successful conversation and a disaster.

The Parts of an Apology

It's not unusual for people to feel hurt even after they've received an apology. Many callers on our radio program worry that they're holding a grudge or are, in some way, being unforgiving because they still hurt after the person who offended them said they were sorry. It's possible these callers are being unforgiving, even if they actually want to forgive the person who hurt them. There's a good chance, however, that the real problem is that the apology failed to convey something the offended person was looking for.

Whether you are on the giving or receiving end of an apology, a good apology consists of three elements:

Feel It

It isn't enough to say "the magic words." The offender has to demonstrate that they genuinely understand the pain they have caused the other person.

Own It

Here's what you don't say when you're apologizing: "I'm sorry, but you shouldn't be so thin-skinned" or "I'm sorry, but I was only kidding" or "I'm sorry, but your expectations are way too high" or anything of the sort.

Comments like these seek to limit the responsibility of the offending party by blaming the offended person. This amounts to a non-apology. It has no power to heal any damage that has been done to the relationship. It implies that the offended person shouldn't take the offense seriously.

A sincere apology acknowledges that the offended party has a right to be hurt, a right to expect better from the person apologizing. For instance, they can rightly expect the person at fault to say something like "You had every right to be hurt by what I did. I'm so sorry that I let you down."

Fix It

A complete apology requires that the offender do whatever is necessary to repair the damage they did to the relationship. A person willing to make restitution never says, "I said I'm sorry! What else do you want from me?" Rather, they say something like "I know that I can't undo what I did, but I want to do whatever it takes to prove that you can trust me again. Can we figure that out together?"

In order for an apology to be complete, an offender needs to be willing to feel it, own it, and fix it, as we say to our callers. If any of these components are missing from an apology, the hurt, anger, and pain of the original injury will likely persist, even if the offended person extends forgiveness.

When this is the case, it isn't because the offended one is being unforgiving; it's because they are being asked to extend not forgiveness but "cheap grace." The Lutheran theologian Dietrich Bonhoeffer, martyred at the hands of the Nazis, coined the term, defining it as, among other things, "the preaching of forgiveness without requiring repentance."[5]

St. Augustine defined forgiveness as surrendering one's natural right to revenge: we give up our desire to hurt the person who offended us or to see them suffer for having hurt us.[6] Sometimes that's a lot, in and of itself. Regardless, the offended person is not required to make things right, especially not on their own. Making things right involves reconciliation, and reconciliation is a process.

Forgiveness is the first step in reconciliation, but these two actions are different things altogether. It's possible to forgive someone but still not be reconciled to them—because, for example, the other person is not sorry, can't be trusted to not hurt us again, or is unwilling to do what is necessary to repair the damage they have done to the relationship. I can forgive someone by refusing to harm them and wishing no harm on them, but I would also be perfectly justified in setting boundaries, or even cutting them off, if that person is unwilling or unable to do the work of reconciling with me.

This distinction between forgiveness and reconciliation is tremendously important, because many of the difficult conversations parents want to have with adult children involve hurts that they have committed against each other. Family members are often put out because someone they hurt isn't willing to extend cheap grace. They expect to say the magic words ("Um, sorry") and then get on with life as if nothing has happened. This, however, is an unreasonable expectation, especially in Christian families.

For the Christian, loving someone means working for their good. Generally speaking, it isn't working for an offender's good to let them off without requiring them to feel it, own it, and fix it. How can they learn and do better? Failing to require an offender to feel it, own it, and fix it could create what Catholics call a "near occasion of sin," wherein the offender feels justified, on some level, in continuing to commit the offense.

Moreover, failing to require an offender to feel it, own it, and fix it tends to fill a relationship with resentment, preventing it from being deep enough to contain important conversations.

True Reconciliation

Many families are terrible at truly reconciling with one another. They expect to cover up offenses—big and small—by saying, "But we're family!" The more a family does this, the more their relationships become a landfill of unspoken resentments and passive aggression. Such families are almost incapable of having effective conversations about anything, especially topics that are important or difficult. There's just too much residual emotional garbage they have to wade through.

Don't be discouraged if you recognize your family in this description. With God you can clean up any mess: no mess is too big for him. Even if you think your family is the emotional equivalent of a superfund site, God can facilitate reconciliation, enabling your family to have effective, meaningful, and even difficult conversations. Here are some ways to cooperate more effectively with his grace.

Bring the Hurt to God

Notice we didn't say, "Give the hurt to God." Why not? Because that implies that we are off-loading our problems on the Almighty and expecting him to sort them out for us. We often hear from clients and callers, "I keep giving X to God, but it keeps landing back in my lap anyway." Exactly.

The point of bringing something to God is not having him do our homework for us. Rather, it's asking him to sit with us and teach us how to do our homework. We bring our problems to God, and when we do, he says, "I'd be happy to help.

Let's go through this together. Show me the first thing you think you should do."

In short, when you bring the unforgiveness in your family to God, don't expect to dump it in his lap and walk away. Expect to invite God into a process. Ask him every day, "Lord, teach me to respond to the pain in my family in a way that glorifies you, works for the good of everyone involved, and helps me be my best self." Then prayerfully reflect on what that means right now for the next step in front of you.

Keep doing this every day. Invite God to help you heal the hurts in your family. He will also use these challenges to draw you closer to him.

Ask Honestly

You can't heal a wound you don't know about. Most parents of adult children feel stiff-armed by their adult kids but leave it alone, telling themselves, "I guess that's just what happens. . ." This is nonsense. Every adult child on the planet wants a good relationship with their parents. If you don't have one, there's a reason.

There's no shame in that, only potential. That's why you need to honestly ask the question: "I love you, and I would like to be closer than we are. Clearly something is coming between us. What do you think I need to do to show you that it's safe to be closer than we are?"

This is a hard question to ask. Often we don't really want to know why our adult kids struggle to be open with us. We may say all the right things: "You can tell me anything." "What's going on?" But we don't really want to know what they think about us, because we're pretty sure the answers will be unfair, unkind, unfixable, or just plain hurtful.

Be not afraid. Whatever the answer is, bring it to God. Trust that he has a process for this, and he will lead you through it.

Listen Openly

Listening openly means listening nonjudgmentally. Your adult kids may indeed answer the "What could I do?" question with a host of unfair, unkind, unfixable, and just plain hurtful comments. That's OK. In fact, take it as a backwards compliment. If your kids didn't trust you, they wouldn't have the courage to dump all this on you.

It may be terribly hard to hear, and much of it may not even seem true from your perspective. That's OK. Don't defend yourself. Just listen openly. Whatever they say, thank them for it. Tell them you really want to think and pray about it, and after you do, you would like to have another conversation, if that's OK with them.

This might seem like a heroically difficult thing to do. And it is. But here is why you need to do it.

In order for your adult kids to feel safe exploring serious issues that are getting in the way of your relationship, they need to know that you are strong enough to face their stories head-on, without flinching (too much). This is a lot like how God handles our anger at him. He knows our anger at him is unjustified, misplaced, and probably completely wrongheaded. But he lets us beat on his chest and scream until we've exhausted ourselves, and then he holds us in his arms and helps us heal. He knows that before we let him heal us, he has to convince us that he is big enough to take our pain. Parents need to do this for their adult children.

Accept What You Hear

Listening openly doesn't mean that we have to agree with what our adult kids say. There will be a time for talking through those differences, if necessary. For now, your adult kids just need to know that you are big enough to hear what they have to say. Then and only then will they know it's safe to work toward the kind of reconciliation that will allow real, meaningful conversations to flow.

Accepting what you hear doesn't indicate agreement. It indicates that you acknowledge that this is where you begin solving the problem. If your house is damaged in a flood, you might not like it, and you certainly wouldn't agree that it should have happened, but accepting reality allows you to start reclaiming your home.

At this stage, try to limit yourself to asking clarifying questions. For instance, instead of defending yourself against what you feel is an unfair attack, you could say, "I really did try to be supportive (or loving or generous and so forth), but obviously I wasn't giving you what you felt you needed. What do you wish I had done differently?" Then listen openly.

Use this basic format as often as necessary. Don't argue about what happened, and you don't need to agree. Simply gather information about how to make the relationship work better moving forward. In fact, as the opportunity presents itself, make sure to ask the follow-up questions: "Even though I can't go back and give that to you, would you like it if I responded to you that way in the future?" And "Are there times it would be important to get that from me moving forward?"

If you feel at all resentful of this process, try to look at it as a spiritual exercise. Allow God to use it to break open your heart a little and heal parts of you that you may not even realize need healing. Keep bringing everything to God and asking him to teach you to respond to whatever your adult kids say in a manner that glorifies him, helps you work for the ultimate good of everyone involved, and enables you to be your best self—the self that can bring out the best in your adult kids.

Respond Lovingly

When you do reengage, preferably after you've cooled down and brought things to God, it's time to respond lovingly. Remember, loving someone means working for their good. You're not going to fight about what really happened, and you're not going to defend yourself. You're going to work for the good of your adult child and the relationship you want to have with them.

That means you are going to use the three-step apology process to address their wounds and move the conversation toward what needs to be done to reconcile. This indicates that you feel the pain they feel, that you wish you had done things better, and that you're committed to helping them meet their needs moving forward. You create a dynamic that allows you and your adult kid to clear the rubbish out of your relationship so that it can be deep enough to contain all the conversations you want to have.

Here's how a client of ours—we'll call her Meredith—used this process to rebuild her relationship with her son.

◆ ◆ ◆

Meredith is a sixty-seven-year-old widow. Her husband, Michael, passed away two years ago. At first her three children were extremely helpful and supportive. For at least the first year, they came around regularly, called often, and helped out whenever she asked.

Eventually, though, Meredith began to feel as if the kids were drifting away. They visited less frequently. When they called, their conversations deteriorated from pleasant to dutiful.

They seemed increasingly resentful of her requests for help. One time her oldest son, who had always been supportive, even yelled at her and hung up on her.

Meredith couldn't understand why her children were being so mean. Couldn't they understand how lonely and scared she felt? Why couldn't they see how hard it was for her to be without her husband, their father? How had she managed to raise such selfish, awful adult kids?

As time passed, her relationship with her adult kids became more and more stilted, superficial, dutiful, and obligatory. They still visited, but the visits were shorter and less frequent, and their conversations more shallow. "I have deeper conversations with strangers," Meredith said. "I don't understand what happened."

We talked Meredith through the process we outlined in this chapter, but it took quite a while before she could work up the courage to follow the program.

She brought her situation to God. Every day she prayed—not just that God would fix things for her, but that he would teach her to respond to the challenges in her relationships with her adult kids in a way that would glorify him, work for the good of all, and allow her to be her best self—the self that could bring out the best in her kids.

After talking with us several times, Meredith felt strong enough to initiate the conversation with her oldest son. Despite his having yelled at her, she felt he might be the most receptive. "I finally asked him the question you told me to ask. I said, 'I'd really like to be closer. Clearly there's something coming between us. What would I need to do to show you that it's safe to be closer than we are?'"

She went on: "He said some of the hardest things I have ever had to listen to. He told me that they all loved me, but the more they helped me and came around, the more 'crippled'—that was the word he used!—I seemed to get. He said that I wouldn't visit them unless they picked me up. That no matter how many times they tried to show me, I wouldn't try to learn how to do little household things like taking out the screens in my windows or flipping a circuit breaker. That I'd just say I didn't know how and wouldn't even try. He said that the more they came around, the more I seemed to live in a bubble that got smaller and smaller, and they felt like they were losing me too.

"I sort of forgot myself and tried to defend myself for a minute. I told him that I do most things for myself, and I could get along just fine. He said that I didn't get it. That I wouldn't drive anywhere I haven't been a thousand times. That I would only have a relationship with them if they could fit into my bubble, and that unfortunately, they were too busy to always accommodate me.

"He said that they pulled back in part because they were hurt that I wouldn't make more effort to meet them places—including his house (never mind that the way I know how to get there is under construction!)—and in part because they hoped that if they were around less, I'd do a little more to 'get a life.'

"I was so hurt. I couldn't believe it. But I did what you said. I thanked him, and I said I wanted to think and pray about it. When I had a chance to take it all in, I'd like to talk again. He agreed, and I hung up.

"I cried so hard. I don't think I had cried like that since Michael died. I felt like I'd lost my whole family. After all the sacrifices I had made for them growing up. Couldn't they see how overwhelming everything was? Why couldn't they just give me a little grace?

"Anyway, I brought it to God the way you said. After a couple of days, I texted my son to ask if we could talk again. I told him that it was really hard to hear the things he said, but that I was doing my best to listen. I said that I didn't want to argue about things, even though I saw them a little differently. Instead, I asked what I could do moving forward to show them that it would be safe for us to be closer.

"He said it was little things, like being willing to learn how to meet them places. Or I could invite a friend to a movie or go out to a restaurant or even go to a bookstore by myself. They wanted to see me trying to live a little more and trying a little harder to come out of my shell.

"To be honest, I've never been a very outgoing person. I tended to rely on Michael to come up with things to do or to drive if I didn't know where I was going. He kind of handled all the things I didn't feel confident doing. When I prayed about it, I had the insight that I was trying to make my adult kids fit into the space Michael used to fill. I was so scared and overwhelmed when he died, I didn't feel as if I could spare the energy to start doing all the things he used to do.

"I still think the kids could have handled it better, but I guess I can see that I wasn't being fair to them. I'm only sixty-seven, for heaven's sake. I guess in their eyes, I was acting like I was eighty-seven.

"I didn't like hearing what they had to say, but now I have a way to start rebuilding our relationships. I asked them to forgive me for giving in to my fears. I told them that I understood how upsetting it must have been for them to feel as if they were losing their mom too, and I promised to try harder to be more outgoing. I was glad to hear my son apologize for yelling at me and hanging up.

"We're going to try to figure out a better way to handle the times when we get frustrated with each other. I'm going to keep talking to them about what I can ask for help with and what they'd like to see me do myself—little household things, for example. I don't really like any of it, but I see their point. The good news is that I can already tell that the kids are trying to reach out more and be nicer. I'm hopeful that this might be the start of a better relationship for us. I just need to keep working the process, I guess."

Although Meredith's situation was unique to her, the process she used to rebuild her relationship and open the previously closed lines of communication with her adult kids is universal. It can be used for any situation that needs healing, forgiveness, and reconciliation.

Remember, in order for meaningful (and especially difficult) conversations to happen, the relationship needs to be deep enough to contain the conversations. If the deepest parts of your relationship are filled with unresolved emotional trash, there is no point trying to engage in discussions. That trash has to be removed first, and the process we outlined in this chapter makes that possible.

We'll leave you with one last tip: you don't have to go it alone. Meredith didn't. She was so tired and frustrated about her relationship with her adult children that she reached out for professional help. Family therapy—even family therapy without other family members—can help tremendously in healing relationships with adult children. If you don't know where to start or your efforts to move things forward keep blowing up in your face, don't hesitate to reach out to CatholicCounselors.com or a local professional to get the support you need.

FOR PRAYER

Lord Jesus Christ, give me the grace and guidance I need to respond well to any hurts, wounds, or offenses that are making it difficult to have the honest, deep, and rewarding conversations I long to have with my adult children. Help me forgive and be forgiven. Show me how to fill the gaps that divide me and my children with your love, peace, understanding, and healing. Amen

Holy Family, pray for us.

FOR REFLECTION

1. Review the components of an effective apology: empathy, acknowledgment of hurt, and restitution. How do these change your understanding of what is needed if you are to seek or extend true forgiveness?

2. How does the distinction between forgiveness and reconciliation change your understanding of what healing your relationships with your adult children involves?

3. How do you think the steps presented at the end of the chapter (bring it to God, ask honestly, listen openly, accept what you hear, and respond in love) can inform your attempts to heal any hurts that make it difficult to have meaningful conversations with your adult kids?

CHAPTER NINE

Support vs. Endorsement

Carol called in to More2Life to ask about her relationship with her adult daughter, Julia, who is thirty-two and living with her boyfriend, Chuck.

"I don't understand why she thinks it's OK to live with him. He's an OK guy. We like him well enough, but we didn't raise her this way. She knows how we feel about cohabitation, but any time we try to bring up our concerns, she accuses us of being unsupportive.

"What are we supposed to do? I want to be supportive of her, but I can't endorse her choices. I feel as if I'm stuck between a rock and a hard place."

◆ ◆ ◆

Carol's quandary is a common one. Our adult children often make decisions we would rather they didn't, and then they're affronted when we express our disapproval. How can we support our children when we can't endorse some—or any—of the choices they make?

The good news is that it's possible to do so. We can even get to the place where our adult children respect our concerns or objections—even if they don't agree with them. Learning the difference between support and endorsement is the key to this outcome.

Begin with the understanding that our adult children don't think they're doing bad things or making bad choices. Even we, when we do bad things, tell ourselves that we have good reasons, that the things we're doing aren't so bad, and that, after all, these things could probably be even good. Now, it's true that when we do this, we're often lying to ourselves, but that doesn't change the fact that we can genuinely believe we're doing wrong things for good reasons.

Based on this, it's possible to say that behind many actions—including irresponsible, upsetting, frustrating, and even some immoral actions—is an attempt to meet a need or express a positive intention.

Now let's go back to the main point. To support someone is to acknowledge and express approval of the *intention or need* that is driving their behavior. To endorse their actions is to approve of both the intention behind the behavior and the behavior itself. Let's illustrate this by returning to Carol's situation.

Carol's daughter is living with her boyfriend. Carol has tried to convince Julia to either stop living with Chuck or get married. Julia has objected to both options and accused her mother of being unsupportive. Carol, heartbroken, wonders how she can be supportive when she morally objects to how her daughter is living.

The answer is that Carol must find a way to separate what Julia is doing (cohabiting) from the need Julia is trying to meet or the positive intention she is trying to express by cohabiting. If Carol can do that, she will most likely be able to validate the need or intention behind Julia's life choices, even while asking Julia to reflect on whether there aren't better ways to meet the need.

For instance, Carol might say, "Can you help me understand why you think living together is the best option for you?" Julia might give any number of answers. She might say that they can't afford to live separately and that they are saving up so they can get married. Alternatively, Julia might say that she and Chuck love each other, but they need to establish themselves in their careers before they're ready for marriage.

In either case, Carol could be supportive of the desire to be financially more secure or the desire to be in a better place in their careers without endorsing the need to live together to accomplish those ends. She could say, "It makes sense to me that you would want some financial security [or career success]. In fact, I want that for you too. But if that's really what you want, living together might actually be getting in your way. Have you ever thought about whether this is really the best way to meet your goal?"

As the conversation progresses, Carol and Julia might be able to have an honest discussion about, for example, the financial risks of living together before marriage. The financial complications can be overt or subtle. Do Julia and Chuck have a joint savings account? Have they bought a house together? Are they in some way supporting one another financially? Is one of them called upon to support the other in a way that is building low-level resentment? Do they argue about finances? Do they discuss their budget and agree on finances?

The fact is, Julia is building a life with someone and making financial decisions with someone who has no legal obligation to honor those commitments. If, God forbid, Julia and Chuck ever break up, what would be the financial toll of extracting herself from the relationship? Could Carol and Julia explore other ways for her to meet her financial goals without having to live with Chuck?

If the issue has to do with their careers, Carol could point out that a big part of a healthy marriage is learning how to balance work life and relationship life. Does Julia realize that they're setting a precedent whereby it's OK for them to choose their careers over each other? How does she think that prepares them for the marriage they'd like to have one day? Would it make more sense for Julia and Chuck to figure out how to fit their careers into their marriage instead of the other way around?

As the conversation continues, Julia might admit that, like most cohabiting women, she would like to be married. However, she's afraid that if she pushes the issue, Chuck will leave, and then she'll be alone.

At this point, Carol can express support by letting Julia know that she understands her fear of being alone. Simultaneously, Carol can ask, "Is hitching yourself to someone who might not be ready for—or might not even want—the kind of commitment you want the best way to address potential loneliness?"

Throughout all these conversations, Carol is not—at least directly—trying to talk Julia out of living with Chuck. She is accepting the fact that this is the way things are for now. But Carol is recognizing that Julia is cohabiting, not because she wants to live an immoral life or reject her parents' values or defy God, but because she is scared. She doesn't know how to meet her needs without making the choices she has made.

Even though it's clear that Carol doesn't endorse Julia's choice, Julia can still receive her mother's support. She can recognize that Carol is taking the time to understand her motivations and to honestly explore other ways to meet her needs.

Needless to say, some of these conversations can be tense and difficult. Nevertheless, this approach makes conversation possible.

Simply saying, "Don't you know that living together is sinful? You need to stop." is a nonstarter. Strictly speaking, the statement is true; but practically speaking, that approach will have little impact on the adult child's behavior. Supporting the positive intentions behind your adult child's undesirable choices—even if you can't endorse the choices themselves—gives you a way to potentially disciple your adult child into making healthier choices.

St. Augustine famously said that we are to love the sinner but hate the sin.[7] We fulfill this dictum when we develop the ability to separate a person's intentions from their actions and then work compassionately with them to find healthier, holier, more fulfilling ways to meet their needs.

What's more, our adult children can come to see our disagreement with their life choices not as a rejection of them but as a concern that they are somehow settling for less. If an adult child objects to this approach, a parent can diffuse the tension by saying something like "I need you to understand that I'm not judging you. I'm trying to say that you deserve the best, and I'm afraid that with this choice, you're settling for less than you deserve. You can be upset with me if you want, but I'll never stop trying to remind you that you deserve all the joys and all the blessings God wants to give you, even when you have a hard time believing it yourself. I love you too much to let you settle for less than that."

No matter how much parents and adult children may disagree, adult children feel supported when disagreements are rooted in the parents' belief that their children deserve the best from their lives and relationships.

Discipleship Parenting

In our books for parents of children and teens, we advocate something we call discipleship parenting. Discipleship parenting is based on the educational and child-rearing principles of St. John Bosco. He encouraged his followers to reject the heavy-handed approaches to discipline that were popular in his day in favor of an approach rooted in reason, religion, and loving-kindness.

How does discipleship parenting differ from conventional parenting? Here's a simple explanation, using the example of discipline.

A more conventional parent says, "My child is misbehaving." The discipleship parent says, "My child is struggling with something that's difficult for them." The discipleship parent honors the child's flawed but sincere attempt to meet their needs, while the parent looks for ways to encourage, teach, model, and support the child in finding a better way. This allows the discipleship parent to correct the child without jeopardizing the rapport they've built. The child experiences the parent's correction as helpful rather than shaming. Discipleship discipline avoids problems associated with either a heavy-handed or a permissive parenting style.

Discipleship parenting is helpful when raising young children, but it's absolutely critical in our relationships with our adult children. Too many parents approach their adult children with the attitude that the kids are misbehaving and that the parents need to unload a stern correction to get them to fall in line. If the adult children push back, the parents need to be harsher and even more rejecting of the children, in order to get their point across. Adult children will always resist this approach. It destroys rapport and undermines our relationships with them.

As Christian parents, our job is always to disciple our children, even when they are adults. We cannot disciple our adult children by criticizing, judging, rejecting, or condemning them.

When we separate our adult children's intentions from their behaviors and help them be their best and pursue the best in their lives and relationships, we're able to guide them without threatening our relationships with them.

This approach means that we can support, not alienate, our adult children and at the same time remain true to our values. Having taken the time to identify the needs our adult children are trying to meet, we can enter into respectful, prayerful dialogue about other ways to meet those needs. Even when our adult children disagree with us, they can feel supported by us. They will see that despite our differences, we really do have their best interests at heart and are working for their good, rather than trying to shame them for making the wrong choices.

FOR PRAYER

Lord Jesus Christ, your mercy knows no bounds. Even when we sin, you see the needs we are trying to meet and our good intentions, and you patiently show us healthier, holier paths. Help us adopt a similar approach with our adult children. Give us the grace we need to avoid shaming them, judging them, or antagonizing them.

Bless us with the wisdom to understand their needs and concerns and the patience to accompany them in their journey to find the healthiest, holiest ways to meet those needs. Amen.

Holy Family, pray for us.

FOR REFLECTION

1. How does the distinction between support and endorsement change the way you think about relating to your adult child who thinks, says, or does things you disagree with?

2. In your opinion, what are some of the needs your adult children are trying to meet when they do the things they do?

3. What small things can you do to support your adult child when you can't endorse the choices they make?

CHAPTER TEN

Fostering Credibility

"My mom hates my boyfriend," says twenty-seven-year-old Marie. "I'm so sick of hearing it. I get it. Sometimes Paul drinks too much, but it's only social—like if we're at a party or something. He's not anything like Dad. My dad would start drinking the second he came home from work and not stop until he passed out in his chair.

"My mom thinks that if I went back to church, everything would be better, but she's gone to church her whole life, and it hasn't helped her or Dad one bit. It's fine if that helps her deal, but I guess we all have to find our own way, you know? I just wish she'd respect the fact that my way is different."

◆◆◆

Luci, thirty-three, has been struggling in her relationship with her parents since the last major election. They now avoid each other, after several vicious fights about their respective politics.

"My parents got really upset with me during the last election, because I hated the candidate they supported. They accused me of abandoning the pro-life principles they raised me with, but I just don't see it. I'm pro-life, but if pro-life means protecting babies before birth and then leaving their mothers in poverty, I don't think that's right.

"I know my folks mean well with all their vote-pro-life stuff, but my whole life, they couldn't say enough bad things about single mothers and their 'bad choices.' They hate the idea of what they call government handouts to people whom they judge to be irresponsible. They think that if you screw up, you need to suffer to learn your lesson.

"I think that's horrible. People aren't perfect. Sometimes they make mistakes. Sometimes bad things happen to them. My parents think those people don't deserve help. I think they do. I have no idea how to square my parents' kind of thinking with the gospel. So yes, I think abortion is terrible, but I'm not going to vote for someone who says he's pro-life and then supports all kinds of laws that make people have to get abortions in the first place. I really don't understand where my parents get off criticizing me. They're the hypocrites, not me."

◆ ◆ ◆

Whatever you think of these two stories, they both point to the same challenge: establishing credibility in our adult children's eyes. Credibility is essential if our adult children are to become willing to engage in serious discussions with us, much less give any weight to the things we say.

We think our children should automatically see us as credible sources of information and counsel because we're their parents. But often they don't. Sometimes, in fact, our adult children know us better than we know ourselves. Sometimes they see things in our lives that cause them to dismiss—or at least seriously question—what we're trying to communicate to them. Those perceptions about our own life choices may or may not be accurate, but we need to be sensitive to the way our adult children view us and be willing to address those perceived flaws.

This can be humbling, but it can be a powerful way for God to use our relationships with our children to bring about important changes in our own life. And if we're willing to do the work we need to do in order to make those changes, then we model that humble, self-correcting behavior for our kids. This can open up new opportunities to move conversations forward.

St. Francis de Sales spoke of people who have what he called an attractive faith—those who live in such a way that others want to follow them.[8] Sometimes, it must be said, we haven't offered our adult children an attractive reason to be open to the opinions, beliefs, or lifestyle we advocate. When this is the case, we shouldn't be surprised that they prefer not to talk with us about a topic or dismiss our attempts to raise issues. We experience this as a rejection, but that's not what it is.

What it can be instead is a judgment of sorts on the kind of witness we're giving regarding certain topics that are important to our adult children. In short, we may be giving credible witness in some areas of life but not in others. For instance, Marie's parents gave a good witness about how to stay together through difficult times, but they didn't give Marie a terrific example of how to have a healthy marriage. Marie isn't rejecting her mother's advice because she fails to love her mother or respect her mother's efforts to maintain a stable home life despite very real obstacles. She's rejecting it because she doesn't believe her mother can offer her credible advice on choosing a good husband or building a healthy relationship from the ground up.

Further, Marie doesn't see her mother's faith as having anything to offer in this regard. Marie's mother may find that a hard pill to swallow, but Marie isn't wrong. If Marie's mother wants to have more influence over her daughter's choice of a mate, she (and ideally, Marie's father too) would do well to enter counseling and attend support groups for problem drinkers and the people who love them. This would not only address a long-standing problem in Marie's family of origin but also increase her parents' credibility in Marie's eyes. She might then be more inclined to see them as a trustworthy source of healthy relationship advice.

In our other example, it's possible that Luci's parents have been more generous than she knows in their attitude toward single mothers and in charitable giving to programs that benefit single mothers. Unfortunately, their words and actions have undermined their credibility. Luci doesn't reject her parents' pro-life stand. But if her parents want to to have more productive conversations about politics with her, they're going to have to demonstrate that they aren't insensitive to the struggles of single mothers.

Growing in Christ

When we speak with parents of adult children about credibility, it's not unusual for them to object that they don't have to prove themselves to their children. Of course they don't. But as Christians, we do need to be open to the possibility that the Holy Spirit is using any variety of means—including conversations with our children—to ask us to grow.

Strictly speaking, we don't have to make an accounting to our adult children any more than they have to make an accounting to us. But we are all responsible to God for the depth of our ongoing conversion and the effectiveness of our witness—even when it's hard to hear negative information about our witness, even when we have to listen very prayerfully, and even when that message comes through our adult children. The Holy Spirit can use them to call us to deeper conversion.

What we're really talking about is the virtue of humility. We're not talking about beating up on ourselves or saying that we or our gifts are of no value. That isn't a virtue; it's low self-esteem.

Pride is the sin of believing that we have all the answers and don't need anyone else to tell us what to do. Humility is the virtue that reminds us of our need for others and our need to be willing to learn from others. Pride inclines us to lecture. Humility reminds us to listen. As such, humility is an important virtue to cultivate if we want to have meaningful and (especially) difficult conversations with our adult kids. In humility we can ask if there's anything in our witness that is an obstacle to the Holy Spirit working through us to reach our children's hearts.

A Painful Path

A recent call on our radio program illustrates this point. Al called to complain about his two adult children, each of whom is cohabiting with their paramour. "I've tried to talk to them a bunch of times about how the way they're living is offending God, but they're not willing to listen to anything I say. We barely have anything to do with each other anymore."

We asked him what he was hoping for from the call. He said, "I'd like some advice on how to get them to be open to me and get their relationships right with God." We sympathized with Al's difficult situation; it was terrifically painful for him.

We asked Al about his own relationship status, knowing how important a credible witness is. Was he married? If not, was he in a relationship? Whether married or dating, what was the quality of his relationship?

"Oh!" he said, somewhat taken off guard. "My wife and I are divorced. The divorce was finalized two weeks ago."

We're not casting aspersions on Al. Clearly his heart was in the right place. He was doing his best to respond to the tremendous pain he and his family were experiencing. Families like Al's (which, let's face it, are like many families these days) deserve nothing but love and support. Nevertheless, it should be obvious to the reader why Al's children were less than eager to receive his relationship advice.

We have friends who have been involved in a national marriage ministry for over forty years. Parents regularly ask them, "What can we do to raise kids who will save themselves for marriage?" Their answer: "Show them a marriage that's worth saving themselves for." Their point is that our witness to our kids is a million times more effective than the words we say to our kids.

Returning to Al, we suggested two things. First, we encouraged him to avoid making his entire relationship with his children about their current life choices. Even when people resist hearing the truths of our faith, they are still open to receiving the love of Christ that we share with them. When we share that love, we can help them, encourage them, and fellowship with them as we are able.

Second, we encouraged Al to get his own personal and relational life in order. Even from our brief conversation, it was clear that there were several layers of pain in his life that he needed to address. We encouraged him to seek personal counseling, during which he could explore the lessons to be learned from his marriage and even explore whether reconciliation might be possible. We encouraged him to seek spiritual direction, in order to more effectively discern what God was calling him to do next.

Finally, we asked him to consider what changes he should make so that his witness to his kids would be even more compelling than his words. That didn't mean that his life had to be perfect. It meant that he needed to show his adult children how his faith was giving him both the strength and the motivation to work toward a healthier, holier life on all fronts. He needed to witness not to perfection but to his powerful effort to struggle in a faithful, consistent way toward a life and relationships that radiated the grace and love of God.

Granted, all this is a lot harder than lecturing our adult kids to straighten up and fly right. But think of the changes that could happen in Al's life if he followed through with our advice. Even if he never reconciled with his wife, learning to support her in a faithful, loving way would be a witness to his kids. Al could demonstrate how his faith motivated him to be a blessing to his kids and their mother under the most difficult circumstances, pushing through the worst of times with humility and courage.

Al could take a horrible situation and allow God to turn it into a sign of his love and power. That would do more to challenge his kids' rejection of his faith than anything he could say. He could become the man they would want to follow.

This path reflects the call to intentional discipleship: wholehearted surrender to the Lord and the desire to be credible witnesses to adult kids. In Al's situation, there's simply no way around it. If he wants to have meaningful conversations with his kids about their relationships, he has to get his own life and relationships in order.

If your adult children are resisting your message, it could be that they're stubborn, but it could just as easily be that there is something about your witness that they believe is inconsistent with your message. Be humble enough to address that inconsistency—perceived or otherwise—boldly and gracefully. You don't have to be perfect before your adult kids will be willing to listen to you, but they have to see you genuinely striving to have your message match your witness. Show your children how to strive humbly, courageously, and gracefully. More important, show them how your faith is what fuels your striving and defines the vision you are pursuing. That will give you the credibility to move toward the more meaningful and difficult conversations you would like to have with your adult kids. It can move them toward love, dignity, respect, and all the virtues that will help them live life as a gift.

FOR PRAYER

Lord, give me the humility to hear your Holy Spirit speaking through my kids' resistance to the things I want to say and the conversations I want to have with them. Help me know what you are asking me to change in my life and relationships so that I can be a more credible witness to my adult children.

Give me the grace I need to consistently strive toward the life you want for me—a life that would inspire my kids to be open to hearing my words and following my example. Amen.

Holy Family, pray for us.

FOR REFLECTION

1. Consider how your adult kids have responded to your attempts to have meaningful conversations with them. What do their responses say to you about how they perceive your witness?

2. What changes would you need to make to effectively address any negative perceptions of your witness?

3. What difference do you think these changes could make in your relationships with your kids?

4. What help or support do you need in making these changes in your life?

PART THREE

Tending the Buds

Having prepared the soil and sown the seeds for good conversations with your adult children, you need to tend the buds that begin to emerge. The final chapters in this book will look at simple ways to keep your relationship flowing smoothly so that you always have opportunities to talk, things to talk about, and the ability to respect the boundaries that help healthy conversations grow. In this section, we'll consider

- how rituals and traditions give your conversations a trellis on which to grow,
- how healthy boundaries prevent us from overfertilizing the conversational seeds we've planted or trampling on the young plants as they blossom and take root, and
- where to go from here.

CHAPTER ELEVEN

Building a Trellis

In order to have meaningful conversations with someone, it helps to have a body of current shared experiences. It isn't enough that you've piled up a host of past shared experiences. You can only talk about the past for so long. If you don't have a host of meaningful, current, and shared experiences to draw from, it's next to impossible to have meaningful conversations with anyone, including your adult children.

This should be obvious, but we're pained to say that it doesn't appear to be so. When parents call our radio program to complain about their shallow relationships with their adult kids, we always ask what they do together. What do they do to connect or spend time with each other? More often than not, the answer is that they have a weekly or monthly phone call, maybe some texts, and a holiday thrown in here and there for good measure.

You might say that this is because, in our very mobile culture, parents and children often live far away from each other. But that's not necessarily the reason for limited contact. When parents and children have good relationships, even when they live far away, they tend to be more intentional about connecting—both in real life and digitally—than parents and children who may live close to one another but have less satisfying relationships.

Shared experiences support meaningful conversations. But the thing is, shared experiences don't just happen. We need to create and nurture them. We can do this, to a significant extent, by establishing rituals and traditions.

In *Parenting Your Kids with Grace* and *Parenting Your Teens and Tweens with Grace,* we discuss the power of working, playing, talking, and praying rituals to bind families together; communicate Christian attitudes toward work, leisure, relationships, and faith; and give families opportunities to work through the challenges that threaten the core of their relationship. In addition to more common rituals of connection, family traditions are a special set of rituals that center around meaningful religious and cultural events like holidays. Both rituals and traditions are critical for keeping families together and making meaningful conversations possible.

Two Families

Imagine two families, *Family A* and *Family B*. Imagine that both families are experiencing some conflict. Family A doesn't have strong rituals or traditions. They know that they should work through their differences, but because they don't have strong rituals that more or less force them to be together, they have to make a special effort to carve out time to address an issue. The problem is, no one really wants to make time to deal with a problem—much less a relationship problem.

Inevitably, despite all their good intentions, the family keeps pushing down the road those important conversations that could get them get back on track. As more time passes, it seems absurd to bring up those divisive issues again. After even more time, this family gets used to ignoring these issues and may not want to deal with them at all. The family connection will most likely devolve until it could be described, at best, as cordial but shallow and somewhat cold. There are too many things to discuss, the time to discuss them seems to have passed, and the effort to dredge it all up again seems too costly.

On the other hand, Family B has worked hard to create strong rituals and traditions. They meet for regularly scheduled family meals at each other's homes. They have regularly scheduled family Zoom calls that involve the adult children who live far away. They play an online game together that has them interacting several times a day. They have a family message group on social media, which allows them all to check in with each other throughout the day and share prayer requests. They get together for holidays, and when some of the adult children are visiting in-laws for those holidays, they schedule a different time for the whole family to be together.

It's understood that all of these things are expected of the family, but rather than holding this expectation over each other's heads, they work hard to be accommodating about how these events come together. They make sure their rituals and traditions are doable.

Because of the effort they put into connecting on a regular basis, Family B, when it has a problem, can't help but deal with it. Family members might be irritated with each other, but they know that they're getting together to have that meal or play that game. This forces them to try to talk things out beforehand because no one likes to deal with emotional tension when they're eating or playing a game. Because they have set up a regular way to pray for each other, they can ask for prayer to get through those conflicts. They don't have to make time to deal with issues—they've already carved out time that allows them to do that.

Because they have established traditions and simple rituals of connection, Family B is more likely to avoid getting off track in the first place and much quicker to get back on track when needed. The connections also give them a shared body of experiences, which enable them to understand each other's points of reference. Rituals and traditions help a family invest in each other and give them a reason and opportunity to keep talking when things get tense.

Keep in mind, however, that adult children are leading their own lives, so it's important to keep family rituals and traditions simple and flexible. If they're married—and especially if they have their own children—they have a biblical responsibility to put their new nuclear family above their families of origin. Healthy rituals and traditions should not make participants feel as if they're wearing chains. Rather, they should serve as refreshing touchstones that allow family members to connect on a regular basis, share experiences that fit into their busy lives, and foster deeper connection with each other.

Staying Connected

Parents who struggle to have meaningful conversations with their adult children tend to assume that families inevitably drift apart in our modern world. On the other hand, parents who are more capable of having meaningful conversations with their adult children work hard to make these connections happen. They don't do this by pressuring and guilting their adult kids into getting together. They simply create the understanding that making time for family is important, and then they find times that more or less work for everyone.

Here are a few examples of work, play, talk, and prayer rituals and traditions that may work for grown families. Family members can participate either in person or online; almost all of these activities can include those who can't be there in person.

Work Rituals

- Helping each other with regular household maintenance.
- Helping each other with special household projects. If a family member needs coaching on how to do something, a video call can work as well as in-person assistance.
- Shopping together for groceries, clothing, birthdays, and holidays. For example, you can discuss a family member's birthday present by video call while shopping online together.

- Planning regular family events together.
- Engaging in charitable service projects together. There are websites that offer ideas for charitable service activities that families can do together, even online.
- Creating a small family business or side hustle, such as making and selling handicrafts.
- Write your own ideas here: _____

Play Rituals

- Playing online games together.
- Regularly playing board games and party games.
- Having family meals together on a regular basis. Distant family members can participate via a Zoom call while they have their own meal.
- Holding a weekly, semiweekly, or monthly family day for adult children. It should be flexible enough to allow for other things that come up.
- Getting together to watch sporting events or other entertainment.
- Write your own ideas here: _____

Talk Rituals

- Have regular family meetings to catch up and keep relationships on track.
- Plan regular one-on-one times to have coffee, breakfast, or other meals or snacks together. For example, plan a

common dessert—you can both order from a bakery that has an online site—and have it with coffee together over Zoom or a similar site.

- Set up a family chat group on social media, allowing for regular check-ins and ongoing conversations.
- Take advantage of texting to send "How's your day going?" or "Praying for you" texts to one another.
- Write your own ideas here: _____

Prayer Rituals

- Attend Mass as a family as often as possible.
- Make daily prayer intentions and requests part of a family chat group on social media.
- Share answered prayers as part of a family chat group.
- Occasionally text prayers for an adult child's day, including blessings or concerns that the child has expressed in the family chat room or in personal conversation. Instead of saying, "I'll pray for you," text an actual prayer. For example: *"Lord, please bless Carla in her job interview today. Help her remember all the gifts and talents you've given her. Help her find the position that allows her to have the life you want her to have. Amen."*
- Plan periodic family praise and worship time, during which you can pray together for individual or family concerns, sing worship songs, and so forth.
- Write your own ideas here: _____

Traditions

- Do holiday preparations together, such as getting the Christmas tree, blessing Easter baskets, shopping for the Thanksgiving meal.
- Have holiday celebrations together as often as possible.
- Celebrate family events together, such as birthdays and anniversaries.
- Attend religious celebrations together. In addition to attending Mass or other liturgical events, consider gettting your family pets blessed on St. Francis of Assisi's feast day, attending Mass together on days memorializing the passing of a family member, and participating in other religious celebrations that have personal or family significance.
- Establish cultural traditions that express your ethnic roots and celebrate your family heritage.
- Write your own ideas here: _____

We've gathered these examples from families we know who connect around working, playing, talking, and praying together and who have established firm family traditions. Granted, it would be the rare family who could do all or even most of the activities, although technology is making things easier than ever. Even so, imagine the family dynamics of those who make a regular effort to do even one of the suggestions in each category. Imagine the conversations that family can have, compared to those of a family who do none of these things.

Families who share rituals and traditions have more to talk about and more reason to talk. Families who don't . . . don't.

As we have said, you cannot force family rituals and traditions. If you do, you may get resentful compliance—at best—but you will not facilitate actual relationships within the family. All your hard work won't bear fruit when it comes to being able to have meaningful conversations. Intimacy cannot occur at emotional gunpoint.

Making It Happen

Rituals and traditions don't happen on their own. There needs to be some intentionality and even some gentle, positive pressure to make these things happen regularly. You can achieve this by first creating the expectation that "we need to do *something* together regularly."

Don't say this in some wistful way—as if connecting as a family is a nice fantasy that will just never happen. Say it in a positive, hopeful "Let's get out our calendars and make something happen" kind of way. You might throw out a few suggestions, but don't force a particular idea. Use your ideas as conversation starters.

Second, generate discussion. Get everyone's buy-in by having them suggest things they would like to do together. Be generous. Don't rule out ideas because they aren't your thing. It's fine to suggest your favorite activities, but the goal isn't necessarily finding the one activity that you all love equally.

Rather, the goal is finding a list of activities you can all reasonably tolerate or even enjoy and that give you an excuse to be in the same place at the same time together so that you can relate to each other. The relationship is primary; the activity is secondary. Encourage everyone to express a generosity of spirit and an openness to try things that others suggest.

Third, make it clear that, although you would love it if everyone could join in, you understand that people are busy, and so it may not be possible. Let everyone know that you will be happy to have these experiences with whichever adult children and their families are available. Create the expectation that everyone will come without pressuring everyone to come.

Fourth, create positive pressure to participate by making the times you get together as pleasant and enjoyable as possible—regardless of who or how many show up. As the siblings and their families talk with each other about what a great time they had, it will encourage more regular participation among those who didn't attend. It will wear down any resistance among the more reluctant without your ever saying a word.

These get-togethers will build emotional capital and make your family bonds stronger. But save big topics or difficult conversations for later. When you have banked enough positive experiences, you can have meaningful or difficult conversations without overdrawing your emotional bank account.

Fifth, be patient. It takes time to create rituals that strengthen your bonds, deepen your connections, and make meaningful conversations flow. There will be missteps along the way. Remember what G. K. Chesterton said, "Anything worth doing is worth doing badly."[9] It's not important to achieve overnight success; it is important to commit to the ongoing process that makes success possible in the long run.

When you think of our metaphor regarding cultivating your family garden, think of rituals as the trellis that allows your family to grow straight and tall. The rituals you share give your family the ability to create common points of reference, get each other's jokes, and finish each other's sentences because you know where someone's going with their story or their line of thinking.

Creating rituals and traditions involves much more than doing nice things together as a family. Almost every family does that, but not all families get the benefits that fully formed rituals and traditions can provide. Creating meaningful rituals and traditions is less about doing things and more about making a common investment in maintaining the quality of your family relationships. The more you work the process, creating and participating in rituals and traditions over time, the more benefits you and yours will reap.

Be patient. Be consistent. Be positive. Build on successes, however tiny they might seem. Tending buds requires patient and diligent work. Tending the buds of your family garden requires even more.

Regardless of where your family is today, trust the process. It works if you work it.

For Prayer

Lord, you gather and nourish your family, the Church, through rituals that bind us together as one. Help my family follow your example. Give me the loving persistence I need to make connecting as a family a priority for all of us, and grant me the patience, compassion, and flexibility to make sure we connect in ways that work for everyone.

Help me tend my budding family garden with meaningful rituals that will allow us to grow and flourish and have the kinds of conversation that make us one in you. Amen.

Holy Family, pray for us.

FOR REFLECTION

1. What rituals and traditions did you have when your children were young? What worked, and what didn't? How might you adapt those rituals and traditions to nurture your relationships with your adult children today?

2. Consider the five categories of connection: working, playing, talking, and praying rituals, as well as traditions. Which type of ritual does your family do best? In which categories might you improve? What are some ideas that you could propose to your adult children in order to strengthen that category or connection?

3. Social media and digital technology make family connections—especially with adult children who live far away—easier than ever. Are you comfortable with social media and other technologies that make digital connection possible? What would you need to do to become more comfortable? How have the ideas in this chapter inspired you to take advantage of the benefits to be gained by virtually connecting with your kids?

4. Of the suggestions we've offered regarding rituals and traditions, which would be easiest to start? How would you get them started? What other ideas or new rituals could you propose that might create more meaningful connections with your adult kids?

CHAPTER TWELVE

The Art of Patience

The Garden, by Arnold Lobel, is a children's book about Toad, who is planting a garden with seeds that his friend Frog gave him. Toad is very excited, though Frog tells him that a garden is hard work. Undeterred, Toad decides to put in the hard work because he wants his seeds to grow quickly.

At first Toad yells at the seeds: "Start growing!" When that doesn't work, he decides that he's scared them, and so he reads a long story to them. On subsequent days, he sings to them, reads poetry to them, and plays the violin in order to get his seeds to grow faster. But nothing happens.

Finally, exhausted, Toad falls asleep. The next day, his friend Frog wakes him excitedly and points to the buds that have begun to emerge from the ground. Toad is relieved. But he says that Frog is right: growing a garden is a lot of work. This is a terrific life lesson that applies well to our topic. There are things you can do to make your relationship with your adult child grow, but you can't force it. You have to do what is necessary, planting and tending your seeds, but then give the seeds the time and space to grow. You need patience.

Patience doesn't mean leaving things to themselves, assuming everything will work itself out in time. This is a common misunderstanding. Patience isn't a passive virtue; it's active. Patience involves stepping away from whatever efforts you are making in order to reflect on what your next steps might be.

If, for example, you're learning a new skill, there comes a point when you have to stop banging away at things and step back, take a look at your progress (or lack of progress), and see what adjustments you need to make moving forward. This ability to step back, reflect, and regroup is characteristic of the virtue of patience.

Parents who become frustrated about their relationships with their adult children tend to fall into two camps. Parents in the first camp practice a false sense of patience that amounts to throwing up their hands in futility, doing next to nothing—because "What's the point?"—and hoping that things will eventually get better on their own. People in this camp will pray about their situation, but their prayer tends to be the hopeless, passive kind we've already discussed: "God, why are my kids so closed off to me? Please fix it."

As we mentioned earlier, God welcomes any prayers we offer, but the most efficacious prayers are those that ask him to teach us what to do. If you define patience as doing nothing, you're likely to forget that God can teach you to do something effective. You'll end up sitting sadly on your hands, hoping for change someday, after God deals with his extremely long to-do list—sometime after ending poverty and solving the latest crisis in the Middle East.

Parents in the second camp ignore patience altogether. Like Toad in the story, these parents are constantly trying to come up with *the big idea* that will make the relationship work *today*, along with the *big conversation!* These parents' hearts are in the right place. But they busy themselves generating ideas and then throwing those ideas out to their adult children, dealing with the incoming rejection and subsequent frustration and going back to the drawing board to do it all over again. They never stop, reflect on what's working, pray for guidance, listen to other people involved, or partner with those people to create something beautiful together.

When we want to have big conversations with our adult children, we might want those conversations to happen overnight. It's hard to wait at all, much less for the weeks, months, or in some cases years it might take to make the relationship deep enough to contain those conversations. We need to return again and again to this question: "Is it enough to say we had a conversation? Or do we want the conversation to be effective and produce actual fruit?"

If you simply want a conversation, regardless of its depth, you can put down this book and keep doing what you've always done. If you want a fruitful conversation, you'll need to practice patience.

If you practice patience as the active virtue that it is, you can use an idea in this book, step back, reflect on your efforts, prayerfully ask God to teach you what the next step should be, listen to others, pray again, and then do the next thing.

When you practice patience, you not only work hard, but you also work smart.

The other thing that patience does in this context is force us to respect our adult children's rightful independence. Sometimes it's hard for parents of adult children to remember that their children are not children anymore. They don't have to listen to us. They don't have to obey us. They have a right to live their own lives, even if theirs is a life filled with bad choices—or at least choices that we disagree with. Every child—especially an adult child—has the right to be treated as a person and not reduced to a project that we are trying to mold or fix.

Patience enables us to resist the temptation to fix our kids. Patience enables us to listen to our adult children, hear what they actually think, understand why they're doing what they're doing, and receive their ideas about what they need from us.

When we are patient, we choose our words and actions with the greatest good of our children in mind. We give them the space they need to figure things out for themselves so that, in time, they will be more receptive to having certain conversations with us.

How do you know when it's time to push a little and when it's time to back off? What signs do you look for while you're trying to be prayerfully patient?

Merging, Distancing, Midpointing

Family therapists know that when a person responds to another person's bid for a stronger relationship, that response serves one of three functions: merging, distancing, or midpointing.

After the dust settles and you see where everyone ends up, then you know if the response has served to bring people closer, increased the distance between them, or brought them to a point somewhere in between.

Here's how it works. Merging behaviors say, "I need you to come closer." These behaviors can be positive or negative. For instance, when your adult child invites you to do something or makes an effort to respond well to your efforts to build a relationship with them, they are engaging in positive merging behavior. But if you don't do a lot together and your adult child feels that it's difficult to get your attention, that child may pick fights with you. Why? Because these fights force you to spend time together and invest emotionally in their lives. God created human beings to need connection; negative connection is better than no connection at all.

Of course, not all negative behavior is merging behavior. Sometimes adult children engage in distancing behavior. They need space to figure some things out on their own. They don't want you to give them answers.

As with merging behaviors, distancing behaviors can be positive or negative. An example of a positive distancing behavior is when a child says, "I really appreciate the fact that you want to help me, but I'd like some time to figure this out in my own way." Negative distancing behavior occurs when your child avoids you, makes shallow excuses for not getting together, or picks fights with you that make you so angry that you have to stay away; you feel that you can't stand being around them.

Arguments with adult children can be either merging or distancing behaviors. You can tell the difference by looking at how everyone acts afterward. If the fight prompts the people involved to draw closer together—to either keep fighting ad nauseam or, ideally, engage in better problem solving—it's a merging behavior. The purpose of the merging argument is to draw you in—albeit in an unpleasant way—and say, "I need more of you in my life."

The best way to respond to arguments that are expressions of merging behavior is to ramp up the rituals of connection and the time you spend creating positive connections. This addresses the positive intention behind merging conflict: emotional engagement and personal investment in the relationship.

When you have been arguing a lot, it can be hard to put energy into the positive side of the relationship, but that's the key to decreasing the number and intensity of the arguments. Connecting in healthier ways meets the unspoken positive desire for deeper connection that is hidden behind the merging argument.

On the other hand, distancing conflict pushes you apart. Distancing conflict ends with everyone avoiding each other because you don't know what to say or how to engage in a productive manner. Distancing conflict tends to be rooted in the adult child's feeling that they are being suffocated, whether or not that is objectively true. It's their way of saying, "I need space to figure this out myself," when they feel their efforts to say this directly have not been heard or respected.

The best way to address distancing conflict is to give adult children positive ways to distance from you. For instance, you might tell them that when they feel they need some space, they can say that directly to you—no argument needed. Or if the relationships have really deteriorated and you find that you're always making the effort to connect, you might refrain from reaching out for a time and let them call you. It will probably take longer than you'd like, but it will happen eventually.

When they do contact you—and however they contact you, whether by text, email, social media, a call, or a visit—make it as positive an experience as possible. As they contact you more frequently, you can take that as a sign that it's OK for you to reach out. But guage the response. If they back off again, you may have jumped the gun. Let them take the lead again.

The last type of response is a midpointing response. Midpointing means, "I'm comfortable going this far but no further." This might happen when, for example, you get together with an adult child for an activity, have a good time, and then try to broach a topic only to be told, verbally or nonverbally, to back off.

It's easy to take an all-or-nothing approach to these interactions. We often hear from parents, "We were having a great time, but as soon as I brought up X, the whole day was ruined." In fact, the whole day was not ruined. Hidden in the adult child's negative response was a clue to what needs to be done to move the relationship forward. The midpointing response really says three things:

1. I want to be with you.
2. I would like more time to try to figure X out on my own.
3. I might be open to your help and input, but only after I see that you care about all of me and know that you

aren't going to turn me into a project by focusing on this one thing.

All for the Good

Midpointing can be frustrating when the parent feels that the promises of deeper relationship and more meaningful conversations are always dangling in front of them but still inaccessible. You find yourself having basically pleasant but superficial moments of connection with your adult child, but there seems to be a good deal of resistance to having deeper discussions. If this is your experience, take heart.

Focus on enjoying the "superficial" time together. Use this to build up capital in the emotional bank account. Try to understand that your adult child is saying that they want to be with you, but they still need space. Invest more time in the relationship. Focus on creating more rituals of connection, and see what happens.

As your adult child feels safe from your intrusion and sees that you are invested in treating them like a person and not a project, you may find that they bring up a topic when you least expect it—maybe even while you're doing that thing that you suggested as a way of investing more time and energy in the relationship.

Scripture tells us, "All things work for good for those who love God" (Romans 8:28). Take a tip from our heavenly Father. Use every interaction with your adult children for the good. Don't discount otherwise positive, pleasant times because they weren't everything you wished they were.

If your adult child wants to spend time with you—even superficial midpointing time—see it as a good sign. They *do* want to be with you. Build on this by making these times together as pleasant as possible, and then double down by creating more midpointing experiences yourself. There is a very good chance that eventually your adult child will ask for your input on topic X—or at least be more open to your efforts to engage the topic if you bring it up because you really can't contain yourself any longer.

Patience allows you to have this big-picture perspective on your relationship and make responses that help you continue moving forward even when you feel that you are running into obstacles. Patience allows you to step back, reflect on the nature of the responses you are getting as you try to build relationship, initiate deeper connection, allow God to teach you to respond in a way that brings out the best in everyone, and make your next move.

Wash. Rinse. Repeat. Let God lead you and your adult children to the place you would like to be.

FOR PRAYER

Lord, help me avoid the temptation to throw up my hands and wait for you to save my family. Give me instead the gift of patience so that I respond gracefully and thoughtfully to the responses I get when I try to make connections with my adult children.

Teach me to respond to my adult children in ways that will bring out the best in all of us. Show me how to build our relationships. Help me remember to step back, reflect, listen, and pray before I act.

Help me use every interaction with my adult children for their good, just as you use the time I spend with you for my good. Amen.

Holy Family, pray for us.

FOR REFLECTION

1. Does the explanation of patience in this chapter differ from your previous understanding of this virtue? How does this perspective change the way you view your relationship with your adult child?

2. Give one example of merging, distancing, and midpointing behaviors in your relationship with your adult child. How might you respond differently to these situations in the future, based on the knowledge you have gained in this chapter?

3. In general, do you feel that your adult child's relationship with you is one of merging, distancing, or midpointing?

4. Name one thing you would like to do to make your relationship stronger in light of the information presented in this chapter.

CHAPTER THIRTEEN

Where to Go from Here and When to Seek Additional Help

It is our sincere hope that you have found this book useful in your efforts to build your relationships with your adult children and have more meaningful (and sometimes difficult) conversations with them.

In concluding, we want to leave you with certain key points. The first, which we have stated repeatedly throughout this book, is that conversation is never about conversation; it is always about relationship. If you have been unsuccessful in having a particular conversation with your adult child, it's not because you don't have good enough conversational techniques. Research shows that when people have a strong connection and good rapport, they tend to forgive conversational faux pas. Likewise, they tend to bounce back quickly when offense is given.

Communication techniques are helpful, but they run a distant second to the quality of the rapport and the depth of the relationship between two people. If you struggle to have certain conversations with your adult children, you need to work on making your relationships deep enough to contain the conversations you want to have.

Second, working on a relationship is not just a preamble to having that conversation; it's actually an important part of the conversation itself. Being willing to suspend discussions about certain topics while working on the relationship with your adult child isn't abandoning your responsibility to tell your adult child the truth or share your hard-earned wisdom. It's saying to your adult child, "You are not just a project to me. I love you as a whole person. I am here for you in all the ways you need me to be. I also respect you enough to give you the space you need to grow into the strong, capable person God created you to be."

This message is, in many ways, the most important part of any meaningful or difficult conversation you might want to have with your adult child. Please don't skip over or dismiss this part of the discussion, no matter how anxious you are to get to the topic you'd like to address.

The tools we have outlined in this book amount to a working definition of the term "accompaniment." Accompaniment is the most important part of discipleship. Through it we build the kind of relationship that can contain the conversations that help us become the people God created us to be.

Accompaniment does not mean smothering a person with your wisdom, whether they want it or not. It also doesn't mean leaving them alone to figure everything out for themselves, while you stand idly by because "really, what can you do?" Accompaniment is ultimately about doing whatever you can, at all times, to strengthen your relationship with a person. You do this not because you want them to do what you want them to do but because you care deeply for them and would like to play a part in helping them figure out who God wants them to be.

The tools in this book will help you accompany your adult children more effectively. Put these ideas into practice, and you will demonstrate that you truly care about your children as persons, not projects. Then you can play an important role in helping them discover what God wants for their lives.

Once you master the tools in this book, you might find that you need additional help. You should consider seeking help if your adult child struggles with addictions, serious mental illness (including depression and anxiety), abusive behaviors in their marriage or family life—whether verbal, physical, or sexual— or serious issues related to their sexual identity. Also look for counsel if your best attempts to use the tools we've presented seem to be making everything worse. The good news is that a faithful professional family therapist can guide you in building a strong relationship with your adult child so that you can accompany them to the resurrection that comes after the cross.

Too often, when our own efforts fail, we tend to think there is nothing more we can do. But coming to the bottom of the toolbox doesn't mean there aren't any more tools. It just means we need to make a trip to the hardware store. There is much more information that we simply couldn't fit in this book—information to help families face specific challenges more effectively and use these tools with more confidence, despite the resistance their initial efforts might produce.

If you feel that your efforts are running into a wall, we invite you to reach out to our team at CatholicCounselors.com. There you can discover how our Catholic telecounseling practice can be of assistance to you. (See the additional resources section for more information about our work and other sources of support.) Let us help you.

Regardless of where you find yourself on this journey, even your most difficult relationships with your adult children can improve with God's grace and your faithful ongoing effort. Every adult child wants to have a good relationship with their parent. Every adult child longs to know that their parent loves them, is proud of them, and wants to spend time with them. There may be problems to address, obstacles to overcome, and wounds to heal in your relationship with your adult child, but it's worth the effort it takes to set out on the healing journey.

Our heavenly Father never gives up on us, and he asks us, as faithful earthly parents, to follow his example, bringing his undying love to our children. That task will require different things from different families, but there is really no more important work you can do.

Our faith teaches us that family life itself is a ministry. It's the place where Christian people learn to love—not just with our broken human love, but also with the love God the Father has for us. We sincerely hope that this book has given you more tools to accomplish this all-important task and that the additional resources we offer will help you find hope and the strength to press on, even in the face of the most serious obstacles.

As we conclude, we invite you to give your family to the care of the Holy Family with the following prayer taken from the Chaplet of the Holy Family:

> Jesus, Mary, Joseph, model for all Christian families, I entrust my family to your care and protection. Bless each member of my family. Help me and the members of my family to love, listen to, support, and accept one another. Encourage us to challenge one another to be compassionate, merciful, and forgiving as we struggle with the difficulties of our lives.
>
> Guide us to seek goodness and holiness in our everyday choices, actions, and attitudes. Encourage us when our faith is weak and when we fail to lead one another to Christ. Make our home a real dwelling place of peace, joy, and love, where you are ever present among us. May we work to uphold each one's dignity, integrity, and unique contributions to the well-being and growth of our family. And when our time on earth is complete, bring us all safely home to you in the company of heaven. Amen.[10]

It is our most sincere prayer that the Lord bless you and your family abundantly. May he be at the heart of all your conversations, may his words be your words, and may your efforts to strengthen and deepen your family relationships be filled with the grace, peace, and love of the Holy Spirit.

Holy Family, pray for us.

Notes

1. Karol Wojtyla, *Love and Responsibility* (San Francisco: Ignatius Press, 1993).
2. Wojtyla, *Love and Responsibility*.
3. The Gottman Institute, "An Introduction to the Gottman Method of Relationship Therapy," https://www.gottman.com/blog/an-introduction-to-the-gottman-method-of-relationship-therapy/.
4. Pope Gregory I, *The Book of Pastoral Rule* (Crestwood, New York: St. Vladimir's Seminary Press, 2007).
5. Dieterich Bonhoeffer, *The Cost of Discipleship* (London: SCM Press, 1959).
6. St. Augustine, *Letter 100*, http://www.newadvent.org/fathers/1102100.htm..
7. St. Augustine, *Letter 211*, https://www.newadvent.org/fathers/1102211.htm..
8. St. Francis de Sales, *Introduction to the Devout Life* (San Francisco: Ignatius Press, 1995).
9. G. K. Chesterton, *What's Wrong with the World* (Mineola, NY: Dover Publications, 1956).

10. Sisters of the Holy Family, "Chaplet of the Holy Family" nazarethcsfn.org/prayer/chaplet-of-the-holy -family.

Additional Resources

Everyone needs a little help now and then. The following resources can help families have more productive conversations about a host of topics.

Catholic Counselors (catholiccounselors.com): Dr. Greg and Lisa Popcak's telecounseling ministry. Work with a faithful, professional, and fully licensed counselor over the phone or via video teleconference to transform your personal, marriage, and family life. We've been helping faithful people like you since 1999. Let us help you live a more abundant, joyful, and peaceful life.

Al-Anon Family Groups (al-anon.org): A nonsectarian organization supporting families who are concerned about a loved one with a drinking problem.

Association of Catholic Mental Health Ministers (catholic mhm.org): A Catholic parish-based organization dedicated to helping people with emotional struggles and families of loved ones with mental illness find support and resources to face their challenges with grace.

Braver Angels (braverangels.org): A nonsectarian organization dedicated to establishing discussion groups that bring conservatives and liberals together, in order to help people with radically different viewpoints find common ground through honest engagement and mutual respect.

Catholic in Recovery (catholicinrecovery.com): A Catholic ministry seeking to assist people struggling with addictions and their families, with support groups and other resources.

Eden Invitation (edeninvitation.com): A Catholic organization that offers accompaniment and support to Catholics struggling with sexual identity issues and the families who love them.

EnCourage (couragerc.org/for-families/): A group for Catholic families who are struggling in their relationship with a same-sex-attracted family member. It is the sister organization of Courage (CourageRC.org), a support group for Catholics who struggle with sexual-identity issues.

The Hazelden Betty Ford Foundation (hazeldenbettyford.org/addiction/help-for-families/family-toolkit): A nonsectarian organization offering support and resources for families with a loved one struggling with substance abuse.

Nar-Anon Family Groups (nar-anon.org): A nonsectarian organization dedicated to helping families who are concerned about a loved one who has a drug problem.

National Catholic Partnership on Disability (ncpd.org): A Catholic organization dedicated to helping Catholics with disabilities and their families.